CHARLES MANSON

CHARLES MANSON

The Man Behind the Murders
that Shook Hollywood

David J. Krajicek

ARCTURUS

PICTURE CREDITS

Getty Images: 10, 14, 32, 43, 51, 61, 97, 107, 113, 116, 128, 132, 137, 174, 182, 188, 197, 202, 221, 223, 232, 248
Shutterstock: 73, 244
Wikimedia: 74

ARCTURUS

ISBN: 978-1-83857-183-2
AD006675US

Printed in the UK

2 4 6 8 10 9 7 5 3 1

Table of Contents

INTRODUCTION

The Snake Charmer

On a July day in 1969, a musician named Gary Hinman sat bleeding from a gun clubbing to the head in his bungalow in a Los Angeles canyon. He was chanting the Buddhist daimoku as three home-invader hippie friends were preparing to take his life. Metronomically, Hinman caressed his prayer beads and mouthed the sing-song Lotus Sutra mantra, seeking calm in the midst of overwhelming dread: "Namu Myōhō Renge Kyō, Namu Myōhō Renge Kyō, Namu Myōhō Renge Kyō . . ."

"That's good," said Bobby Beausoleil. "Keep it up, Gary."

This condescending encouragement came from the 21-year-old leader of a kill team dispatched to Gary's home from a commune at an old western movie ranch nearby. Beausoleil and two women, Mary Brunner and Susan Atkins, arrived late on a Friday night, following false rumors that their friend was holding vast sums of money.

They were instructed to offer Hinman two options: turn over the loot or die. Beausoleil phoned the ranch for further orders when Hinman swore that he was broke. Twenty minutes later, two men barged into the house, ironically lifting Hinman's hopes that he might be rescued from the madness. Hardly.

The new arrivals included a tiny man of simian appearance, with sable-colored hair and beard and manic little black eyes. Ominously, he was carrying a sword.

Within minutes of arriving, he slashed a gash into the left side of Hinman's head as the confused victim begged to be told why he was being targeted.

His diminutive assailant then rifled drawers, finding just coins and petty cash, before conferring with Beausoleil and fleeing in Hinman's Fiat station wagon. He was leaving the other three to finish the job.

Glib Jailbird

The slasher was Charles Manson. At age 34, he was a glib jailbird who had emerged from prison three years earlier and stumbled into San Francisco as American ingénues in peasant dresses—runaways, hitchhikers, and lost souls trying to find themselves—were streaming into town for the Summer of Love. His timing was impeccable. The patchouli-scented sexual revolution created a perfect Petri dish for his predation. Using prison-honed talents as a con man and his middling skills as a guitarist and singer-songwriter, Manson soon began building a cult of as many as 35 young hippies, three-quarters of them women.

He would spin campfire lectures for his stoner clan, featuring trite college Psych 101 tutorials about projection and reflection. His enamored followers, none of whom would have been mistaken for an intellectual, mistook his dime-store dogma for deep thinking. He basted their brains in a mix of Jesus Freakiness, Dale Carnegie hucksterisms, Norman Vincent Peale's sunny-sided platitudes ("You are perfect!"), and the buggy self-help triangulations and "dynamics" of his prison-library Scientology.

They believed he was a mystic. The writer David Dalton, who wrote the first long profile of Manson for *Rolling Stone*, nailed Manson in eight words: "If Christ came back as a con man." Joe Mozingo of the *Los Angeles Times* drew another vivid analogy: "He was a scab mite who bit at the perfect time and place."

Multiple mugshot of human chameleon Charles Manson during his trial in 1969—he kept changing his appearance but the eyes remained the same.

Using the playbook of pimps and cult leaders, he isolated troubled young women from their past lives and controlled their bodies and minds. He was the Wizard of Oz for libertines, and he as much as told them so. Susan Atkins, who became one of Manson's most prolific robot killers, said Manson often mocked his own followers' blind faith: "He said, 'I have tricked all of you. I have tricked you into doing what I want you to, and I am using you, and you are all aware of that now, and it's like I've got a bunch of slaves around me.'"

Racist and Sexist

Manson was an enigma on so many levels. His enduring infamy as an object of both fascination and revulsion springs from his ability to mind-control his acolytes. He was imbued with the old-timey gender and racial sensibilities of his Appalachian upbringing. In other words, he was a racist and a sexist. He preached female subservience and racial segregation, and his followers lapped it up amid a flowering civil rights movement and on the cusp of the women's liberation movement. In 1969, the debut of *Ms.* magazine was just two years distant, and it would be just three years before states began ratifying the Equal Rights Amendment. Yet Manson's women happily subjugated themselves.

Fifty years after Charles Manson's shocking grand entrance as an American true crime icon, this book looks back at how such a murderous mess by a ragtag collection of hippies and hangers-on could have transpired. It delves into the farcical thoughtlessness and naivety of these young men and women who marched along behind their buckskinned faux-Jesus. I let them try to explain themselves—sometimes to comic effect—in their own words, from transcripts of courtroom or grand jury testimony, recorded interviews with attorneys and the media, and the memoirs and letters many have written.

Blind Faith of Followers

Leslie Van Houten, who was raised in a churchy family in a middle-class L.A. suburb, was an exemplar of blind faith. At age 19 she stuck a knife into the flesh of another human being—which, along with strangulation, is the most tactile and intimate form of murder—simply because Manson told her to do so. She had nothing to gain but little Charlie's validation.

Facing her comeuppance months later, Van Houten sat down with a defense attorney named Marvin Part, who tried to tease some sense out of her. Part asked: "You said something about thinking Charlie is or was Jesus. Do you still believe that?"

"Yeah, I still believe he is," Van Houten replied. "And, you know, I can't say it in words. Only that he's almost not even human. I mean, you know, he's got his body and all, but he's gentle. I mean he's everything. He's just everything at once. It's hard, you know, I can't even almost explain him. And it's like he has no ego. Do you know what ego is? It's faces that we put on for each other. And he has none of that. He's just a person. And, well, it's so hard to explain why I believe he is, but I know he is."

The attorney asked whether Manson claimed to be Christ.

Van Houten replied: "He used to say, 'I see too much; I see what's happening, and I don't want it; I don't want to be in this position.' . . . He'd say, 'I know that I died on the cross before.'"

This seemed reasonable to Van Houten and her doe-eyed cult sister wives.

Manson must have been thinking of Van Houten when he said: "You can convince anybody of anything if you just push it at them all of the time. They may not believe it 100 percent, but they will still draw opinions from it, especially if they have no other information to draw their opinions from."

Killings "Had to Be Done"

Just 29 months after Manson began assembling these naïfs into a communal Family—"heartless, bloodthirsty robots . . . sent out from the fires of hell," as a prosecutor would describe them—they carried out a series of proving-ground murders over four weeks in the summer of 1969 that have endured for half a century in America's fabled pantheon of crime spectacles. The slayings of pregnant actress Sharon Tate, coffee heiress Abigail Folger, Leno and Rosemary LaBianca, and five others in four separate acts of casual savagery remain today a peerless mashup of celebrity, sex, cult groupthink, and bloodlust.

"It had to be done," Van Houten explained. "For the whole world's karma to be completed, we had to do this."

David Dalton had an unimpeded view of that sort of acute palaver during a series of visits, including many overnight stays, at the Manson Family commune. After making his mark at *Rolling Stone*, the London native has gone on to a successful career as a biographer of musicians, including Bob Dylan, Janis Joplin, and Jim Morrison. A self-described "unreconstructed hippie," he lives on a farm in upstate New York—a fine venue for a commune, as he points out.

He was not surprised when I reminded him of Van Houten's explanation that the murders simply "had to be done" for the

In their own bubble: Susan Atkins (l), Patricia Krenwinkel, and Leslie Van Houten laugh in the face of their death sentences for their part in the Tate–LaBianca killings ordered by Charles Manson.

good of cosmic karma. "This cult was like a lot of other groups of people that are so tuned into each other, picking up every vibe, because they were living in a state of constant paranoia and hysteria by that point," Dalton told me.

He called Manson "the perfect storm" for 1969.

"It was the conflation of mystical thinking, radical politics, drugs, and all these runaway kids fused together," Dalton said. "The world seemed to be in a death spiral of violence, and we thought the whole hippie riot was about to begin to save us all. We were going to take over and everything would be cool. In fact, the opposite was happening, embodied by Charlie Manson."

Suburban Kids Playing a Role

The first manifestation of violence fell upon poor Gary Hinman. Years later, Susan Atkins wrote: "The senseless, callous nature of this killing will never cease to grieve and dumbfound me." Her remorse was badly belated. Here's the thing: Hinman did not die easily, despite two deep stab wounds to his chest inflicted by Bobby Beausoleil. The fact is, long before her dumbfounded grief, Atkins held a pillow to her friend's muzzle to stop his breathing. And this is the same Manson automaton who hissed, "I feel nothing for you, woman!" as Sharon Tate begged for the life of her fetus.

The Hinman murder, largely overlooked in the lurid story of the Manson Family, set a standard for brutality that the subsequent violence merely copied. These were not hardened criminals. Most were southern California suburban kids whom Manson had schooled in theft and other make-a-buck petty crimes. But they were not the stone-cold bad asses that Atkins' behavior toward Tate might suggest. They were just playing a role for Manson. Until Hinman was killed, the Family had spent two years focused on sex, drugs, and rock and roll (with excursions into auto theft). Before Manson "got on his 'Helter Skelter' trip," according to Paul Watkins, another follower, "it was all about fucking."

White Album "Messages"

Manson preached a homespun version of liberation theology—the freedom to be you. Yet he felt oppressed by the music industry. He desperately wanted to be a rock star, and he seethed when his unlikely music connections—including Dennis Wilson of the Beach Boys—failed to help him secure a record deal. A switch was flipped in the fall of 1968, when the Beatles released their White Album (officially entitled *The Beatles*). Manson wore out the grooves in the record, and he convinced his followers that the world's most famous band was sending him direct messages in the lyrics, including those of "Helter Skelter." He imagined that Paul McCartney's song presaged a race war that would induce the Family to retreat to California's Death Valley to ride out the violence, then emerge heroically and install Manson as a world leader and master breeder. (Yes, it was that absurd.)

Manson began to recast his horny young stoners into a classic apocalyptic cult, prepping for the end times. Growing impatient for the race war, Manson decided to "show blackie how to do it" by committing a series of murders and leaving behind clues meant to implicate the Black Panthers, the African American political organization that was the subject of America's ever-evolving moral panic of the moment. The starry-eyed plan was a failure on every level. It did not touch off a race war, nor did the murder victims pony up the cash Manson needed to fund his desert fever dream.

The Year When Everything Changed

The implausible story of Charles Manson cannot be separated from the context of its era. It was, by turns, an inspiring and terrifying time as Americans were asking essential questions about what their country ought to be. The half-decade of 1965 to 1970 saw ghetto riots, the emergence of a vibrant new psychedelic culture, shocking political murders, riveting space exploration, escalation of the conflict in Vietnam, and burgeoning war protests. By itself, 1969 featured an astonishing mashup of news events, political intrigue, technological advances, and cultural phenomena that still resonate today. The 1968 assassinations of Martin Luther King Jr. and Robert F. Kennedy, and the attendant rioting and finger-pointing, left Americans on tenterhooks waiting to see what might come out of 1969. The answer: Just about everything.

Events that year seemed to portend glory, calamity, or both. Catastrophes arrived by land, sea, and air. In January, just after Richard Nixon's presidential inauguration, an undersea oil well suffered a blowout off Santa Barbara, California, spewing oil for 11 days and fouling the coast while coincidentally helping to promote the modern environmental movement. Then in June Cleveland's Cuyahoga River, awash in industrial chemicals, caught fire. The year was bookended by meteors crashing to earth in Mexico and Australia.

With 33,000 American soldiers already killed, the count of U.S. troops in Vietnam peaked at 543,000 in late April, two months after Nixon had made secret plans to bomb Cambodia. Later in the year, journalist Seymour Hersh broke the story of the massacre at My Lai, and 250,000 protestors marched against the war in Washington, D.C. ("An effete corps of impudent snobs," spat Vice President Spiro Agnew, who wielded a thesaurus as his political sword.) Across the Atlantic, Charles was invested as Prince of Wales, and British troops were dispatched to Northern Ireland to quell dissent.

The twin Mariner spacecraft completed fly-bys of Mars, beaming back close-ups of the Red Planet. And as *Star Trek* ended its original broadcast run, NASA slid into the captain's chair with a series of thrilling missions in preparation for the July moon shot. (David Bowie killed the buzz a bit with the release of "Space Oddity" a week before: "Your circuit's dead, there's something wrong. Can you hear me, Major Tom?")

New technological marvels seemed to emerge weekly: the first temporary artificial heart and human eye were transplanted 18 days apart in Houston, Texas; the first Internet message was transmitted to a UCLA professor's computer; the first ATM was installed at a bank in suburban New York City; and federal authorities declared birth control safe. In May, a teenager in St. Louis, Missouri, died of a medical condition that would go unexplained until 1984, when "Robert R." was identified as the country's first confirmed case of HIV/AIDS.

Levi Strauss began selling bell-bottom blue jeans, Paul McCartney married Linda Eastman in London on March 12, and John Lennon, not to be upstaged, married Yoko Ono eight days later and tucked into their bed-in for peace in Amsterdam. Construction of Walt Disney World began in Florida, skin-

and-sex *Oh, Calcutta!* opened Off Broadway, and *Sesame Street* premiered on television. Fifty million people watched Tiny Tim wed Miss Vicky on *The Tonight Show.*

In the midst of this came the extraordinary series of events in the summer of 1969, starting with June 28, when a police morals-squad raid on the Stonewall Inn, a gay bar in New York's Greenwich Village, touched off three days of rioting—and ignited the gay rights movement. Then on July 18, Ted Kennedy, surviving male heir to the American political tragi-dynasty, fled the scene of a fatal car wreck on Chappaquiddick Island, Massachusetts. A couple of days later, on July 20, the world watched on TV as Neil Armstrong and Buzz Aldrin took their stiff, bouncing strolls through moondust. Among the viewers was a small group of friends and kin gathered at the home of Sharon Tate. Twenty days later, on August 9, four members of the same group would be savagely murdered by Charles Manson's second kill team. A week after that, more than 400,000 people endured organizational bedlam to attend the Woodstock Festival, 100 miles (160 km) north of New York City in Bethel, New York. That same weekend, Hurricane Camille pounded ashore on the Gulf Coast, east of New Orleans at Pass Christian, Mississippi, killing 256 people.

The Day the Sixties Ended

Does a narrative thread of the Sixties bind these events together, or were they a random, unrelated cluster of data points? Joan Didion, who wrote about Manson in the title essay of her book *The White Album*, portrayed L.A. as a timorous place occupied by paranoiacs huddled behind triple-locked doors. "Many people I know in Los Angeles believe that the Sixties ended abruptly on August 9, 1969," she wrote, "ended at the exact moment when word of the murders on Cielo Drive [at the Tate house] traveled like brushfire through the community, and in a sense that is true. The tension broke that day. The paranoia was fulfilled."

The juxtaposition of the Manson murders and the peace-and-love vibe of Woodstock days later made the shock seem psychedelic, sunflower orange swirled into purple amethyst. Manson revealed the cankerous underbelly of the tie-dyed, rosy-spectacled era. Had the Sixties vibe been nothing more than ganja smoke and mirrors?

I asked a writer friend, John Kincheloe, for his perspective. A history teacher and musician, he was living in a rural niche of the counterculture in 1969. John and his twin brother, George, were 19-year-olds from Pittsburgh who had just finished their first year of college in Massachusetts—John at Williams, George at Harvard—and were working as dairy farmhands in the northeast. John recently published a memoir about his trippy experiences that summer, centered on an excursion to Woodstock with his twin brother and friends. I asked Kincheloe about the loss-of-innocence trope concerning Manson and the Sixties. He said:

As I look back on those times, I think that they already were "ruined" by the brutal assassinations and race riots. Those events gave me a sense that, even before that summer, this country had somehow slipped into a great hole of wretched violence, including the widespread brain-dead support for the war in Vietnam. All of these things were so totally foreign to the sweet

*peacefulness and security of my childhood in Pittsburgh that I
thought then that an ugly turn had taken place at the moment
JFK was murdered in Dallas . . .*

*The Manson business really just seemed to be unconnected
to the youth movement I felt a part of just by being alive and
19. I remember thinking that there must be a lot of fucking
crazies in California for such an asshole to get that many people
to listen to him.*

One of those crazies was Paul Watkins, who in his own memoir
addressed the question of what exactly he was searching for when
he stepped into Manson's commune. "More than anything," he
wrote, "I wanted to identify more closely with my inner processes
and the cosmic forces which seemed so inaccessible in the wake
of a civilization gone mad. What the youth in America were
looking for in the late Sixties, it seemed to me, was a shared love
and a sense of identity."

Practiced Manipulator

The Sixties created Manson, and his crimes were an exclamation
point to a turbulent decade. He also helped snuff out the
emerging hippie movement in its infancy. Manson was no hippie.
Instead, he was a cynical ex-convict who manipulated hippies—
the embodiment of flower power gone to seed.

A charismatic snake charmer who told his audience
what they wanted to hear, Manson spoke or wrote a million
words about his life and crimes—in court, in letters, in media
interviews. But although he bleated many excuses for his wasted
life, almost always beginning with a lack of parenting and proper

education, he showed his true nature while facing murder charges. He sacrificed his loyal hippie minions to save himself, claiming they had acted on their own, not at his bidding. The talons of his psychological claws went so deep that most of them guilelessly agreed that Manson was blameless, even as they faced condemnation to the gas chamber.

Manson played crazy, but that was just another studied tactic. As Vincent Bugliosi, his prosecutor and biographer, said before he died in 2015: "His moral values were completely twisted and warped, but let's not confuse that with insanity. He was crazy in the way that Hitler was crazy. He's not crazy. He's an evil, sophisticated con man."

Manson died in 2017 without having uttered a word of regret. Susan Atkins, his illustrious sexpot murderess, had a moment of realization about Manson before her own death from brain cancer in 2009. She produced a memoir that was sharply critical of her former sage and lover.

> *In hindsight, I've come to believe the most prominent character trait Charles Manson displays is that of a manipulator. Not a guru, not a metaphysic, not a philosopher, not an environmentalist, not a sociologist or social activist, and not even a murderer. His long-term behavior is one predominantly of a practiced manipulator.*

She called him

> *a liar, a con artist, a physical abuser of women and children, a psychological and emotional abuser of human beings, a thief, a dope pusher, a kidnaper, a child stealer, a pimp, a rapist, and*

a child molester. I can attest to all of these things with my own eyes. And he was all of these things before he was a murderer.

This might have seemed obvious to any perceptive adult who entered Manson's orbit in the late 1960s. As we will see in this look back at Manson's life and crimes, Atkins arrived at her bracing conclusions far too late to save nine fellow human beings.

CHAPTER ONE

A Lost Childhood

A mid the wordy froth of his deflective New Age psychobabble about reflection and projection, Charlie Manson occasionally managed to summon up an elemental truth about himself that hinted at self-awareness. He once said, for example: "I am a child of the '30s, not the '60s." His psyche was molded not by the Age of Aquarius but from the scars of a dismal childhood that began near the nadir of the country's most trying economic crisis.

Teenage Mother

He was born at Cincinnati General Hospital in Ohio on November 11, 1934. Five years after a catastrophic stock market crash announced its arrival, the Great Depression had made itself at home in the United States by the date of Manson's birth. Half of the nation's banks had failed, and a quarter of all able-bodied men and women were out of work by 1933— nearly 13 million people from a 52 million-strong labor force. Millions more were underemployed. Across the country, food lines snaked through the streets of great cities and humble towns alike. Halfway through his first term, President Franklin Roosevelt had helped institute New Deal initiatives to create jobs and protect the welfare of the least among the citizenry, but recovery came slowly, in fits and starts.

Few American children have begun life under more dire circumstances—both national and personal—than that boy born in Cincinnati. His mother, Kathleen Maddox, was an unmarried teenager who was walking a crooked path through life. The youngest of three children, she was raised by strict Church of the Nazarene parents, Nancy and Charles Maddox, in Ashland, Kentucky, an Appalachian river town at Kentucky's convergence with Ohio and West Virginia. It was a morally conflicted corner of Appalachia, where rough-and-tumble coal miners lived cheek-by-jowl with Bible Belt holy rollers.

"Her parents loved her and meant well by her, but they were fanatical in their religious beliefs," Charles Manson told biographer Nuel Emmons. "Especially Grandma, who dominated the household. She was stern and unwavering in her interpretation of God's will and demanded that those within her home abide by her view of God's wishes."

Religious strictures could not confine Kathleen. Her childhood—and her innocence—ended early. By age 14 or 15, the petite girl was hanging out with rugged men at Ritzy Ray's, a beer joint across the river in Ironton, Ohio, a foundry town that served as the region's sin city. Many Manson biographers have described his mother as promiscuous, and some say she was a prostitute, but Manson pushed back against characterizations of his mother as a "teenage whore." On the other hand, he told Emmons: "In later years, because of hard knocks and tough times, she may have sold her body some."

Absentee Father

He never met his father, a Ritzy Ray's regular named Colonel Walker Henderson Scott. Scott was not a military man; his occupations, including mill worker, railroad laborer, and bar room custodian, generally do not come with that swaggering honorific. In fact, Colonel was his given first name—a hopeful cadge of a title long bestowed on accomplished Kentucky dignitaries (and certain fried-chicken magnificoes). Colonel Scott lived in Catlettsburg, Kentucky, just downriver from Kathleen's hometown and Ironton. He was 24 years old and Kathleen was 16 when she got pregnant, but he took no interest in his act of procreation. As her pregnancy progressed, Kathleen took the somewhat traditional American route of leaving town to escape the hometown shame of unwed motherhood, traveling 150 miles (240 km) to Cincinnati, where she gave birth. Charles Milles Manson's first and middle names were given in tribute to his maternal grandfather, who had died three years before the boy was born. His surname came from William Manson, a laborer whom his mother married at about the time her child was born. He was gone from their lives nearly as quickly as Colonel Scott, but the name stuck.

Struggling to raise her child alone, Kathleen soon returned to Ashland, where her mother and grandmother helped care for the boy. She filed a bastardy lawsuit again Scott, in 1936, and the following spring Colonel Baby-Daddy was ordered to pay a meager monthly fee to support the child. He treated the order the same way he had treated parental obligation: He defaulted.

Manson's rudderless, parentless upbringing became a central feature of his id. He raised the subject again and again as the chief excuse for his personal failings. Any hope he harbored to meet his biological father expired in 1954, when the heavy-drinking Colonel Scott died of cirrhosis. Kathleen was not a nominee for mother of the year. She flitted in and out of his life—mostly out—as she had an itch for sex, alcohol, and quick money. When Charlie was just beyond toddler age, his mother and her older brother, Luther Maddox, were arrested for a stick-up in Charleston, West Virginia's capital city. The details suggest the robbery was planned after a long day in a tavern: The siblings poked a rigid object into the back of their mark, an acquaintance named Frank Martin. Only after he had handed over $35 did he see that the weapon was a glass condiment container. A story in *The Charleston Daily Mail* called it a "ketchup bottle hold-up," but a judge was not amused by their choice of weapon: He sentenced the brother and sister to five years in prison in 1939.

Locked Up for the First Time

Little Charlie was on the move again, farmed out to an aunt and uncle—Kathleen's sister Glenna and her husband, Bill—in McMechen, West Virginia, a city in a far-off northern corner of the state, 225 miles (360 km) from his Kentucky kin. McMechen's location had one advantage in that it was just a few miles from the state penitentiary in Moundsville. Charlie spent his first time behind bars there, in the visiting room with his mother.

Kathleen was paroled after three years, in 1942, just before Charlie's eighth birthday. Her parenting skills had not improved in prison, and her free-range son was already earning a reputation as an incorrigible truant and quick-fingered thief. Kathleen tried to make a fresh start in Indianapolis, where she had another relative, an aunt. But the change of venue did not fix her alcoholism and other mothering deficiencies, so young Manson was placed in a series of foster homes in West Virginia and Indiana. The authorities tried without success to force him to attend school, and he gave up on formal education in 1943, as a nine-year-old third-grader.

Four years later, at age 13, he began a long life behind lock and key when he was turned over to the Brothers of Holy Cross at Gibault School for Boys in Terre Haute, Indiana. The stern Catholic priests who ran the reform school did not spare the rod. According to Al Hunter, a local historian and author: "Punishment for even the tiniest infraction included beatings by either a wooden paddle or a leather strap." Manson escaped the reform school at least twice, and while on the run in 1948 he committed his first adult-style crime, cleaning out the cash box during a burglary at an Indianapolis grocery store. That crime and others led Manson into the Indiana School for Boys, a stout juvenile prison near Indianapolis that held the state's hard cases. Manson, a pipsqueak at age 14, later said that he was frequently beaten and sexually assaulted by larger, stronger teenagers there.

Redemption Failure

While he seemed to suffer very real trauma at the School for Boys, Manson also began perfecting a woe-is-me con based on his lousy childhood. Shortly after arriving in Indiana, he had convinced the state children's bureau authorities that he preferred foster care to the profligate lifestyle of his mother, who had been arrested for adultery. "I didn't want to stay where mother lived in sin," he sniffled. (He also found it easier to get one over on foster folks than his own mother.) He used the con on an Indianapolis parish priest he met at the School for Boys. Steven V. Roberts of *The New York Times* reported the remarkable anecdote in December 1969, in one of the first detailed profiles of Manson:

> *Young Manson came under the attention of the Rev. George Powers, a local priest. "This particular boy seemed very lonesome, just craving attention and affection," recalled Father Powers . . .*

"He looked like an innocent altar boy, and he was so ashamed of his mother."

Father Powers arranged for Manson to be sent to Boys Town near Omaha, and the Indianapolis newspaper ran a big story. "He won everybody over," the priest said. "The juvenile court judge was completely taken with his personality. He had ability beyond his years to present himself; he was a beautiful kid for his age."

The *Indianapolis News* portrayed Powers as an angel of redemption for a "dead-end kid."

Its story ran on the front page on March 7, 1949, under the headline: "Dream Comes True for Lad; He's Going to Boys Town." Manson embarked on the 625-mile (1,000 km) journey to Father Flanagan's famous home for wayward boys, located far from temptation out in the country just west of my hometown of Omaha, Nebraska. He mustn't have enjoyed the climate, because his dream stay lasted just four days. Then he ran away from Boys Town and headed back east on a stolen motor scooter that he traded up for a stolen car. Out of money, food, and gas, he was arrested during a grocery store hold-up in Peoria, Illinois. He was bundled back to the Indiana School for Boys, a certified failure at youthful redemption.

Chain of Custody

But the state reform school could not hold him. He escaped several times, intent on making his way to the golden Pacific shores of California. In 1951, he and two reformatory pals in yet another stolen car got as far as Beaver, Utah, robbing gas

The well-turned-out young man who didn't turn out so well: Three days before he ran away from Boys Town, a smirking Charles Manson poses in suit and tie.

stations as they made their way across the country. After that arrest, Manson's next stop in an endless chain of custody was the National Training School for Boys, a federal juvenile prison in Washington, D.C. A psychiatric evaluation there hinted at Manson's gift for deception: He was judged to be "slick" and "aggressively antisocial." But a shrink added that Manson was "an extremely sensitive boy who has not yet given up in terms of securing some love and affection from the world."

Manson wheedled a transfer in 1952 to a less-restrictive "honor camp" in Natural Bridge, Virginia. But as his scheduled parole date drew near, he was charged with raping another teenage inmate at razor-point. That led to two more years of confinement, first at a federal reformatory in Petersburg, Virginia, where his disciplinary record included eight offenses, of which three were "homosexual acts." He was next transferred to one of the federal government's maximum-security juvenile prisons, in Chillicothe, Ohio. By law, he could have been held until his 21st birthday, on November 11, 1955, but he was released early, in May 1954, on credit for good behavior—despite his long disciplinary record. The government then turned him over to the supervision of his aunt and uncle back in McMechen, West Virginia. He arrived there at age 20, having spent the entirety of his teen years in a juvenile reformatory or on the run after an escape.

Short-Lived Marriage

On January 17, 1955, eight months after his parole, Manson married Rosalie Willis, a waitress he had met months before in nearby Wheeling, West Virginia. She got pregnant that summer with a son who would bear his father's name. But the new daddy would prove to be a fabulous failure as a paterfamilias. Manson drove his pregnant wife to California in a stolen car—a federal crime because he crossed state lines. Employing his silver tongue, he got off with probation but was arrested in Indianapolis in March 1956, for failing to appear at a court hearing on another car-theft charge. His mouth couldn't save him that time and he was sentenced to five years in jail and confined at Terminal Island, a federal prison at the Port of Los Angeles. He was handed his first set of adult prison stripes at about the time his son was born in April 1956, but his young wife did not wait for him. Their divorce decree was signed by a judge in September 1958, the same month that Manson was paroled from Terminal Island.

From Auto Theft to Pimping

The young criminal was catholic in his car-theft choices. His first target was a Packard hearse, which he took joyriding when he was 13 years old. Over the years, his hot rides included a 1948 Chevrolet, a 1950 Studebaker, a 1951 Mercury, and a 1952 Cadillac. Having fully explored that crime niche, he stepped up his game following his release from prison, turning away from auto boosting toward pimping and financial crimes. Immediately after he was freed, he began building a small stable of prostitutes, including Leona Stevens, a teenager from Colorado who went by the name of "Candy." (Manson would later marry her as a legal strategy.)

He was arrested in Los Angeles after cashing a U.S. Treasury check for $37.50 that he had swiped from the mail. Manson had a chance to get off easy, once again, after pleading guilty. A weeping Candy swore her devotion to him and begged a federal judge not to lock him up. The judge fell for it, ordering ten years of probation and a suspended prison sentence if Manson managed to live lawfully. That did not happen. He drove Candy and another woman to New Mexico and Texas "for purposes of prostitution," a violation of the Mann Act, a federal sex-trafficking law. When one of the women was arrested on a local sex-for-sale charge, Manson again found himself on the federal hook. The judge revoked his suspended sentence and sent him to prison, where he would while away another seven years of his life—most of it on McNeil Island, a federal prison accessible by ferry, west of Tacoma, Washington.

Young Criminal

Let's pause to regard Charles Milles Manson's early-life crime biography with proper awe. I have been writing about criminals since the 1970s and have researched the rap sheets of many hundreds of bad men and women, both amateurs and professionals, from marquee mobsters to serial killers to common crooks, but I know of only a handful of criminals who stepped so quickly from one crime mess to the next at such a young age. One who comes to mind is Willie Bosket, a legendary New York City juvenile criminal from the 1970s who was an incorrigible delinquent by age nine, a double-murderer at 15, and a prison lifer at 17. Neither Bosket nor Manson was clever at crime, despite all their practice; the better class of criminals doesn't get caught as much. Both men had nightmare childhoods that featured sexual abuse—Manson in reformatories, and Bosket at the hand of his own grandfather.

Grade A Communicator

Experts suggest that young criminals who suffer psychological fissures during childhood crave attention—whether positive or negative. Some say certain crimes can be viewed as a primal scream by a person who is unable to otherwise express anger or anxiety. But most teenagers are impulsive, aggressive, emotionally volatile, and reactive to stress, according to experts like Dr. Laurence Steinberg, a psychologist at Philadelphia's Temple University. Many are sensation-seekers who overlook long-term consequences in favor of short-term payoffs.

A lack of moral grounding and proper education also played a role for Manson. Lynette Fromme, who as Manson's most avid acolyte knew him as well as anyone, said he struggled to read and write. Manson acknowledged his lack of schooling many times, and he was proud of his ancestral ties to old-time Appalachian stock. His hillbilly heritage was manifest in a mountain-talk accent that was more a grating rat-a-tat than a strolling southern drawl, but women found his hillbillyness charming. Fromme said Manson was a "grade A communicator," despite a vocabulary that was "colorful but limited" and an "unruled" comprehension of grammar. His manner of speech was an attention-grabber, standing out from the flat California accent.

Courtroom Monologue

Manson had no compunction about discussing his crappy childhood and early delinquency. No father/no mother was his personal mantra. One example would come during his murder trial in 1970, when he surprised everyone—including the judge, the prosecutor, and especially his own defense team—by declaring that he wished to give testimony. The judge cleared the jury from the courtroom and allowed Manson to make a statement. He spoke extemporaneously for about 75 minutes. Facing capital punishment, he clearly wished to explain how he had become a man widely portrayed as a self-made monster.

His monologue showed rare glimpses of reflection and self-analysis. The statement captivated his young prosecutor, Vincent Bugliosi, an unknown, 35-year-old DA's back-bencher when he was handed the case. As Bugliosi later wrote: "He rambled, he digressed, he repeated himself, but there was something hypnotic about the whole performance. In his own strange way he was trying to weave a spell, not unlike the ones he had cast over his impressionable followers."

Manson said "a lot of things said about me" needed to be "cleared up and clarified." Some excerpts:

I have spent my life in jail, and without parents. . . . I never went to school, so I never growed up in the respect to learn to read and write so good, so I have stayed in jail, and I have stayed stupid. I have stayed a child while I have watched your world grow up, and then I look at the things that you do and I don't understand . . .

I don't think like you people. You people put importance on your lives. Well, my life has never been important to anyone . . . I know that the only person I can judge is me. I judge what I have done and I judge what I do, and I look and live with myself every day. I am content with myself. If you put me in the penitentiary, that means nothing because you kicked me out of the last one. I didn't ask to get released. I liked it in there because I like myself. I like being with myself.

But in your world it's hard because your understanding and your values are different. These children that come at you with knives, they are your children. You taught them. I didn't teach them. I just tried to help them stand up . . . I have killed no one and I have ordered no one to be killed. I may have implied on several occasions to several different people that I may have been Jesus Christ, but I haven't decided yet what I am or who I am. I was given a name and a number and I was put in a cell . . . My father is the jail house . . .

I have ate out of your garbage cans to stay out of jail. I have wore your second-hand clothes . . . I have done my best to get along in your world and now you want to kill me, and I look at you and I look how incompetent you all are, and then I say to myself, "You want to kill me, ha, I'm already dead, have been all my life!" I've lived in your tomb that you built. I did seven years for a thirty-seven dollar check. I did twelve years because I didn't have any parents . . .

You made me a monster and I have to live with that the rest of my life because I cannot fight this case. If I could fight this case and I could present this case, I would take that monster back and I would take that fear back. Then you could find something else to put your fear on, because it's all your fear. You look for something to project it on and you pick a little old scroungy nobody who eats out of a garbage can that nobody wants, that was kicked out of the penitentiary, that has been dragged through every hellhole you can think of, and you drag him up and put him into a courtroom. You expect to break me? Impossible! You broke me years ago. You killed me years ago . . .

Hippie cult leader, that is your words. I am a dumb country boy who never grew up. I went to jail when I was eight years old and I got out when I was thirty-two. I have never adjusted to your free world. I am still that stupid, corn-picking country boy that I always have been.

Wanted to Stay in Prison

In June 1966, four years before he sat in the witness stand rationalizing his life, Manson was transferred from one federal waterside prison to another—from McNeil Island in Washington state back to Terminal Island in an industrial port complex at the southernmost finger of Los Angeles. The transfer was an administrative move in preparation for Manson's parole, scheduled for early 1967. His release produced an often-repeated anecdote that he mentioned in his court statement: He claimed that he asked if he could stay in prison. Manson described the scene for author Nuel Emmons:

I had spent seven years of my life looking forward to the day when I would get out. I had dreams and plans, but as I was being processed for release, I knew the dreams would never materialize and the plans were nothing more than wishful thinking. I'd had my releases before. With me, nothing had ever been as I imagined it. There is a big difference between illusion and reality, and neither was a stranger to me. Since I had at last found a comfortable atmosphere in prison, the streets were not the place for me . . .

I told the officer who was signing me out, "You know what, man, I don't want to leave! I don't have a home out there! Why don't you just take me back inside?" The officer laughed and thought I was kidding. "I'm serious, man! I mean it. I don't want to leave!" My plea was ignored.

Released and Reborn

So on March 21, 1967, Charles Manson once again stood squinting in the sun outside a prison, a freshly minted parolee holding an acoustic guitar and outfitted with the government's traditional going-away gratuities of 30 bucks and an unfashionable suit. The tiny man was prematurely wizened at age 32, having spent most of those years locked up. He recognized that his prospects for going straight were even more remote this time, and he had no one to turn to—no friend or kin in California who would or could take him in. A prison pal, also newly paroled, had invited Manson to join him in San Francisco, and after a couple of days in L.A. he took him up on the offer and hitchhiked 400 miles (640 km) north to the Bay Area. It was a providential decision. That spring, thousands of seekers from across America—vulnerable and trusting "beautiful people"—were streaming into Haight-Ashbury for the 1967 Summer of Love.

Charlie Manson would be waiting for them with his arms wide open.

CHAPTER TWO

Flower Power

T he pop song that helped launch a patchouli-scented horde toward Haight-Ashbury in 1967 was written as a promotional contrivance. John Phillips, bandleader of the Mamas & the Papas, had partnered with Lou Adler, his record producer, to stage the Monterey International Pop Music Festival in 1967. They hoped the three-day event, the first of its kind for rock 'n' roll, would validate that genre in the same way that festivals had helped legitimize jazz and folk in the 1950s, including an annual gathering of the jazz tribe that began in 1958 in Monterey, California. Phillips and Adler chose the same venue, the 20-acre Monterey County Fairgrounds, 100 miles (160 km) down the coast from San Francisco (and 300 miles [480 km] north of L.A.). They booked a line-up that leaned toward psychedelia, with Jefferson Airplane, the Grateful Dead, The Jimi Hendrix Experience, Eric Burdon and the Animals, and Janis Joplin's band, Big Brother and the Holding Company.

But the 33-band schedule also included many major radio hit-makers of the era, including the Association, Johnny Rivers, Simon & Garfunkel, the Byrds, Otis Redding, Buffalo Springfield, and The Who. Phillips' own band was scheduled as the close-down act.

Despite a strong line-up, Phillips and Adler fretted that the event would flop. Their primary concern was attendance, not finances. They faced a minimal payroll because most of the acts had agreed to play for expenses, without performance fees. Tickets were cheap—$6.50 for a seat, $3 for standing room. But the festival had been organized on the fly, over just a few months, and as the June 16 opening date approached, the promoters were concerned about lack of publicity outside of California. Phillips

Three members of the Mamas & the Papas at a press conference in 1967—Denny Doherty, John Phillips, and Michelle Gilliam. To their left in shades is Scott McKenzie. Cass Elliot, the missing Mama, had been unavoidably detained on a charge of alleged larceny.

wanted to make a statement about the popularity of rock 'n' roll, and that meant filling the fairgrounds with 10,000 people for each of the five four-hour schedule blocks over the three days. Six weeks before the Association was due to open the event, Phillips sat down for 20 minutes with a guitar and pen and paper to sketch out a song that he hoped would serve as a pop-radio advertising jingle for the festival. The cinematic opening lines he wrote that day would forever define the hippie zeitgeist:

> *If you're going to San Francisco*
> *Be sure to wear some flowers in your hair.*

Phillips rushed the song into Adler's studio, where it was recorded by Papa John's childhood friend and fellow folkie Scott McKenzie. The wax was still warm when the song was released for radio play on May 13, a month before the festival opening. "San Francisco" was an immediate hit, not only in the U.S. but abroad, going to No. 1 in the U.K. and most of Europe. Its final line was pollen to buzz-chasing hippies from across the hemisphere: "If you come to San Francisco/Summertime will be a love-in there."

The Monterey event, standing in the warm reflected glow of Phillips' lyrics, was a rousing success. Some 50,000 young people found their way to the fairgrounds, and McKenzie— backed by the Mamas & the Papas—sang the new hippie ode before a swaying mass as the next-to-last tune of the festival. Nonetheless, Phillips and Adler had to fight to try to bring the event back to Monterey in 1968. The local blue hairs were not happy about what they saw as an invasion of immorality. Six months after founding his weekly music magazine, Jann Wenner wrote a gritted-teeth account of the controversy in *Rolling Stone*, saying that "an ugly collection of voyeuristic 'taxpayers'" had alleged that the first festival "resulted in sale of pornographic literature, trafficking in narcotics, an invasion of 'undesirables,' and 'open fornication' (with photographs to prove it)." In the end, the blue hairs won. There was no Monterey Pop sequel, but rock 'n' roll prevailed in the long view. Monterey became a blueprint for future festivals, including the iconic gathering three years later across the country at Woodstock.

The Song that Promised Utopia

Haight-Ashbury became a national hippie haven, thanks in no small measure to the summoning lyrics of John Phillips' promotional song. Not long ago, Graeme Ross of the *Independent* called "San Francisco" "the ultimate hippie anthem and a record that more than any other contributed to the aura of the Summer of Love." That is true. It is also true that the cloying flower-power message obscured an uglier reality on the streets of the city.

The song helped impel an estimated 100,000 utopia-seeking young people toward San Francisco in 1967. Most of them descended on the Haight, where early-arriving counterculturalists were already stacked like cordwood in the neighborhood's three-story Victorians. Some were holdovers from the Beat Generation surge, but many were drawn to the city for another seminal 1967 event, "The Human Be-In," on January 14. It was held a couple of miles from the Haight at the Golden Gate Park polo field. Billed as "A Gathering of the Tribes," the Be-In attracted 30,000 hippies and staked a flag for the counterculture in San Francisco.

The event featured performances by several San Francisco bands that would later play at Monterey, including the Dead and Big Brother.

And it included hours of political speeches. Timothy Leary, the acid-advocating psychologist, famously urged the crowd to "tune in, turn on, drop out."

He was joined at the microphone by Beat poet Allen Ginsberg, who chanted mantras, Dick Gregory, the African American comedian and social critic, and Jerry Rubin, the political activist, among others. News photos and film from the event gave many corners of the country a first look at a youth revolution unlike any that had gone before.

Backlash Against Flower Children

Mr. and Mrs. America were scratching their flat-tops and flipped bobs over the San Francisco convergence, and many newspapers and magazines sent correspondents to suss out what exactly happens at a happening.

Despite its reputation as a welcoming counterculture hive dating to the beatniks—a word coined in 1958 by local newspaper columnist Herb Caen—most San Franciscans eschewed berets and daddy-o Van Dykes, including a large loud-and-proud bloc of conservative Roman Catholics. Republican Dwight Eisenhower had carried the city in the 1956 presidential election, although the political balance began to tip toward Democrats shortly thereafter. (Today, registered Democrats outnumber Republicans by nearly nine to one there.)

In the summer of 1967, liberals and conservatives alike were nettled by the drain on city services as a thousand flower children poured in every single day. Joe Dolan, a Bay Area radio host, worried that his town was being cast as a refuge for flakes in stories written by the wave of reporters who followed closely on the heels of the hippies.

> *Now, certainly these shaggies and hippies with their talk about peace and brotherhood and understanding and international amity, all this ridiculous nonsense. Naturally, the newspapers are going to play up the things they say, especially when these people bang tambourines and, like Allen Ginsberg, go into these absurd chants, these Hindu chants. Well, naturally they're going to play this sort of thing up. It would be absurd to expect that they're not going to do this.*

Hippie Otherness Mocked

Rummaging around in a news archive, I found scores of stories from the late 1960s that, as Dolan predicted, played up the otherness of hippies. Most journalists painted a composite portrait mocking them as freaks—lazy, dirty, unemployable, embarrassments to their parents. In one example from June 1967, newspaper columnist Ellis L. Spackman was dispatched to spend two days in Haight-Ashbury, so he could cast his gimlet eye on the hippies. A clever writer, here is how he began one story in his series:

> *Just 1,557 years ago, some 30,000 Goths stood before the walls of Rome, and the Senate and citizenry trembled. On Aug. 24, 410 AD, the Eternal City fell to the barbarians.*

At the present moment, 100,000 hippies are converging on the city of San Francisco, and the city fathers are doing some first-rate trembling. By Aug. 24, the city will have doubtless capitulated and be in the throes of its Summer of Love.

The only resemblance between the Goths and the hippies is that neither of them shave, or cut their hair, or bathe too frequently. There the similarity ends. The Goths wanted to make war, and the hippies want to make love.

The Roman city fathers didn't have to do any planning. The Goths took care of that. But in San Francisco, the municipal authorities have to figure how to pad the unsolicited convention down and how to feed the conventioneers, most of whom will be broke on arrival.

Spackman was not exactly a hick. He wrote for the *San Bernardino Sun-Telegram*, based an hour east of Los Angeles amid the endless suburban sprawl that became known as the Inland Empire. In retrospect, his sharp focus on the otherness of the young people flocking to San Francisco is illustrative.

On close inspection, I regret to say that the Flower Children are a pretty ratty bunch. Perhaps they aren't really dirty, but they certainly manage to convey that impression.

They generally shuffle and shamble and are slumped over. And the expression on their faces seemed bored and vacuous. They may have been turned on and tuned in, but they certainly looked dropped out.

Perhaps this hasty conclusion is unfair, but we looked in vain for symptoms of alertness and intelligence. Altogether it

*appeared as though a lot of young misfits had found each other
and moved off into a strange, sloppy world of their own . . .*

*Suppose you live in Keokuk, Iowa, and have a son who is
an obvious misfit or oddball, who is driving you half crazy. He is
the laughingstock of the high school and you are getting pitying
glances from all your friends.*

*Isn't it better to let him thumb his way to San Francisco
where he can be with others of his ilk and not clutter up the living
room? A mere $50 or $100 a month will keep him eating and
you can say that he "has a job" on the Coast, or "is working" out
there. Perhaps San Francisco has become the national baby-sitter
for grown-up infants.*

Hungering for a Purpose and a Place

Like most of his contemporaries, Spackman missed the true
story of Haight-Ashbury because he was focused on the looks
and comportment of "oddballs." His myopia dulled his ability to
sense the tremors of a cultural earthquake. In a book published
a few years after Spackman had his yuks, Dr. David E. Smith of
the Haight-Ashbury Free Medical Clinic offered an informed
view of the trend that journalists had missed—a concept made
newly cogent by today's rampant opioid overdoses. Smith
and his collaborator wrote: "People use and abuse drugs not
because they are criminals but because they are in pain." He
said many of his patients in the Haight were tormented by a
lack of self-worth, family conflicts, and an inability to fit in
back in their hometowns—the otherness that Spackman had
mocked. Writing about the book for *The New York Times*, the

young journalist Steven Roberts described these young people as "drifters on a tide of indifference, hungering for a purpose and a place."

That describes any number of the Manson acolytes, none more so than Susan Atkins. Born in 1948, she grew up an hour south of San Francisco in San Jose. The middle child of three, her world was upended at age 15 when her mother, Jeanette, died of cancer. She claimed that her father, Steven, was an alcoholic who did not cope well with the death of his wife, so she and her two brothers were farmed out to relatives. A chronic runaway, she was often at odds with her father, who soon remarried, and she spent her coming-of-age years bouncing from one house to another. On her own by age 18, she said her dark side, including a propensity for substance abuse, reflected her dad's problems with booze.

Atkins was destitute and despondent while living in San Francisco in 1966, after failing to scrape by with a difficult job selling magazine subscriptions over the telephone. She then turned to illicit means of support, traveling to Oregon and Washington with two ex-convicts. They were charged with a series of crimes, including robbery, car theft, and possession of stolen property. Atkins got off easy—a few months in jail and probation—and then returned to San Francisco, where the lithe brunette employed her good looks in her next job, as a topless dancer. But that occupation seemed to deepen her despair. She turned 19 in May 1967, a week before "San Francisco" began playing on the radio, beckoning flower children to join the "gentle people" in the city where she was stripping for leering businessmen.

Dressed to kill: Suspects Susan Atkins (on the left) with Patricia Krenwinkel, and Leslie Van Houten outside court in 1969.

Mesmerized by Manson

Atkins said she was a heavy drug user (and occasional seller) by the time she met Manson late in 1967, according to a transcript of a debriefing with an attorney, Paul Caruso. She also admitted to suicidal thoughts not long before the chance meeting with Manson at a crowded commune flophouse on Lyon Street in Lower Haight. She said she climbed to a rooftop while high on acid and asked God to "just stop the world and take me off of it." That changed when she met Manson.

Atkins said she was "mesmerized" when Manson walked into her house with a guitar and began singing and playing "The Shadow of Your Smile," the jazzy ballad that was the theme song of the 1965 film *The Sandpiper*. Nearly every woman who was drawn into Manson's circle said she was immediately captivated, and many claimed a mystical connection. Several said Manson seemed to be reading their mind. During grand jury testimony, here is how Atkins described her Manson moment—a touch of Mary Magdalene meeting Jesus Christ:

> *I was living in a house that primarily consisted of young people living together. We all shared our means of support, and I was sitting in the living room on the first floor of the house and a man walked in and had a guitar with him and all of a sudden he was surrounded by a group of girls. Well, I sat and I watched and he sat down on the couch and I sat down to his right and he started to play music. First he just started playing familiar songs and went through Spanish—a couple of Spanish songs and sung a few songs, and then the song that caught my attention most was "The Shadow of Your Smile," and he sounded like an angel . . .*

And when he was through singing, I looked up at him and I asked him if I could play his guitar, and I wanted to get some attention from him. I don't know why, I just felt I wanted some attention from him and he handed me the guitar and to myself I thought, "I can't play this," and then he looked at me and said, "You can play that if you want to." Now, he had never heard me say, "I can't play this." I only thought it.

So when he told me I could play it . . . it blew my mind because he was inside my head and I knew at that time that he was something that I had been looking for. I didn't know what it was I was exactly looking for, but he just represented something to me inside, and I went down and kissed his feet. I don't know why I kissed his feet, I just kissed his feet . . .

There's a good word to describe what she was feeling—and what many of her Manson Family sisters would experience in Manson's presence: *frisson*, from the French term for shiver. For an extreme example, think of the teenage girls simultaneously shrieking and crying uncontrollably at early Beatles concerts. The emotional and physiological frisson effect in music is a warhorse subject in the academic world of psychology. This condition, commonly called musical chills, is often accompanied by piloerection—goose bumps—which is why Günther Bernatzky, a clever Austrian psychologist, dubbed it a "skin orgasm." So what was Susan Atkins feeling as she listened to Manson's intimate performance? The hairs on the back of her neck stood at attention, and a tingling sensation descended down her spine from the base of her skull, settling into her groin. Frisson brings on a pleasing hormonal surge—an endorphin rush. Academicians call it "a transcendent, psychophysiological moment of musical experience." In other words, temporary euphoria.

Seduction Music

In a 1970 jailhouse interview, *Rolling Stone*'s David Dalton asked Manson: "What makes you such a hot lover?" He replied: "You spend 20 years in jail playing with yourself, a woman becomes almost an unbelievable thing to you. It's like a man in the desert, he's been in the desert for 20 years, and then he comes across a glass of water. How would you treat that glass of water? It would be pretty precious to you, wouldn't it?"

Paul Watkins, a talented musician who was one of Manson's male followers, makes an important point when he says that most analysts of the little man's grip on women have failed to include music as a key factor in his seductions. In his memoir, published a decade after his Family years, Watkins described the first time he witnessed Manson's musicianship:

Charlie took another hit from the joint, then began to sing. He bent forward, hugging the guitar, his hair hanging over his face; he really leaned into the music with body and voice. And he was good, damn good, timing the notes and modulations with a loose-jointed, natural rhythm. Manson had soul and there was genuine merriment in his manner, a contagious style that got everyone off. As a musician I admired his talent for improvisation; it gave the music vitality. Plus, it was right up my alley, 'cause that's the kind of music I do best and that's why Charlie and I connected so well that night.

Those who have written about Manson have always implied that drugs and sex were his primary means of programming the Family. But music was perhaps even more influential. No other art form better expresses and transmits the nuances of the soul. While Charlie was never a great instrumentalist, his voice was strong and he has a good range. He could wail, croon, and get funky. That night he was lighthearted and full of love.

Susan Atkins was feeling the love as she spontaneously stooped to kiss the stranger's dirty feet during her own first encounter with Manson. And she apparently was still buzzing with frisson when Manson returned to the house a day or two later. In her debriefing with attorney Caruso, she gave a blow-by-blow account of a seduction that was quick and quirky, with a kinky twist.

He said do you want to go for a walk with me and I said yes. I felt really privileged because all the girls in the house were just in love with him, his whole mannerism and the way he spoke. And we walked about two blocks away from where our house was to the place where he was staying in San Francisco, and he took me into his room and said, "I want to make love with you," and I said OK. [He asked], "Have you ever made love with your father?" I said no. He said, "Have you never thought about it?" And I got kind of embarrassed and said yeah, like two or three times. He told me to take off my clothes. I took off my clothes. There was a full-length mirror in the room and he said notice yourself in the mirror. I couldn't look at myself. He said, go ahead, look at yourself in the mirror—look how beautiful you are. I looked and I turned away, and he pushed my head back and said, "Look, you're perfect." And I said well, yes, it's okay and while he was making love with me [he] told me to imagine I was making love with my father to get me through that particular hang-up that I had about my father. And about then we were through. It didn't last long. It was better than I'd ever had it before. It was the most beautiful experience I'd ever experienced.

Growing Harem

Atkins was soon riding in a black school bus as a member of Manson's growing harem, which at the time also included Mary Brunner, Lynette Fromme, Patricia Krenwinkel, and Ella Jo Bailey. (Manson gave most of the women new names or nicknames, another mode of control. Atkins became Sadie Mae Glutz, Krenwinkel was rebranded Katie, and so forth. Generally, I will refer to them by their true names.) Attorney Caruso, flummoxed by this arrangement, asked Atkins to explain what they were doing. The answer probably scuffed his wingtips.

She explained: "We were just all together in the bus going through our changes, getting to know each other, getting uninhibited so we could make love to each other freely. And he [Manson] put me through a few changes with Lynn, and he would make love with Lynn and I'd feel jealous, and so would everybody else in the bus for the simple reason he always picked her. In all three years he only made love with me six times."

Caruso responded: "That's strange. You're a very attractive girl."

"Thank you," Atkins said. "I'm aware of that."

CHAPTER THREE

The Master Manipulator

While spending the first seven years of the Sixties locked up, Manson listened with wide eyes when fresh prison arrivals gave him news about the wondrous cultural metamorphosis going on beyond the walls. He described how it felt to suddenly find himself at the epicenter of the changes, days after parole:

> *Frisco and the generation that now occupied its streets was something else. While in the joint, guys would mention, "Man, if you been locked up since 1960, you ain't going to believe the changes out there." And they would describe all that was happening in the Haight-Ashbury district of San Francisco and across the bay in Berkeley. For that matter, the whole generation, everywhere, would be an extreme eye-opener. I believed some of it but wrote most of it off as just more convict bullshit. But, man, they weren't lying. Some mighty big changes had taken place since I had last been on the streets . . . I felt I was in a horse-and-buggy trying to keep up with a jet-liner.*

He got up to speed quickly, finding the free-love lifestyle to be a convict's dream. At first he slept in parks, and then he stepped up to backyards, living room floors, and couches as his street-corner serenades opened doors to hippie flops in the Haight. Those connections led him across the bay to Berkeley, where musicians often gathered to jam for tips on the University of California campus.

First of the Many

It was there, just a few weeks out of prison, that a dog approached Manson and gave him a wary sniff. He began chatting with the owner, a 23-year-old woman from Eau Claire, Wisconsin, who

Mary Brunner after her arrest for using a stolen credit card at a Sears store the day before the Tate murders.

had recently moved 2,000 miles (3,2000 km) to take a librarian's job at Cal-Berkeley after earning a history degree back home.

"The girl was a slim, red-headed, straight-laced type," Manson said. "She wasn't pretty, but . . . she had qualities."

Her name was Mary Brunner, and she invited Manson to stay at her apartment that night—an act of compassion, not sexual invitation. But she fell under his thrall after a week or so, and became his very first initiate. The relationship quickly got complicated as she was forced to learn to share her new beau with other women—lots of them.

Favorite Acolyte

Lynette Fromme came second, a month after Brunner, although she would become his favorite. As night fell one May evening in 1967, Manson approached her on L.A.'s Venice Beach while on a trip to southern California with friends. She was a petite redhead and a budding hippie, wearing a paisley dress adorned with two pendants hanging at her breast—a raw walnut and an old skate key. Fromme was at a vulnerable moment that day. Just 18 years old, she was a community college freshman from nearby Torrance, and she had endured a fraught relationship with her stern aeronautical engineer father. He thought Lynette was lippy and disrespectful, and for several years they barely spoke—in part because William Fromme cruelly forbade his daughter from occupying any room he was in.

They had had a fresh argument that May day, and it ended with her father decreeing: "Get out of this house and never come back." She then thumbed a ride to Venice Beach, where she found herself "left in the dark, completely alone." As she wept, Manson suddenly materialized before her, wearing a smuggler's cap, a flight jacket, and blue jeans. He hopped up on a wall beside her and said: "Name's Charlie." She says she freaked out when he suddenly declared: "So your father kicked you out."

Once again, he seemed to be reading her mind. She described her first impressions of Manson in a memoir published in 2018—shortly after his death, not coincidentally. She did not need to worry about his reaction; the book is an admiring portrait that reveals her as an unreconstructed fan.

> *He moved with smooth confidence. He appeared both big and small. I was enchanted yet flustered . . . He had a cleft chin and a Southern country accent I would later recognize as typically West Virginian, more a strum than a twang . . . I was most arrested by his eyes. They knew me. He was a present and active intelligence. I didn't understand it. I didn't know what made his face a comfortable place to rest my eyes . . . He knew something about being trapped, he said, because he'd only recently been released after seven and a half years in prison . . .*

Just minutes after they met, she followed him into a car bound for San Francisco—and never stopped following. As she got to know him on the long car ride, she found him to be "a combination of

Charles Manson's two "for-ever-girls," Lynette "Squeaky" Fromme and Sandra Good (holding her infant son Ivan Pugh), at a preliminary hearing in Los Angeles, December 1969.

braggadocio and self-realization." She added: "The attraction was disconcerting. Something about his moves and casual postures made him interesting to watch."

Manson took her home to Brunner's apartment. He played his guitar and sang for the two women, then crept into Fromme's bedroom on an after-midnight ramble. "As I expected, he came in, put his arms around me, and I, in my actions, said yes-no-yes-no with a history of old movies in my mind and no intention of giving in at all," Fromme wrote. "He gently pushed me away from him; I pushed him back. He laughed, but said, 'Who do you think you're fooling?' and walked out of the room."

Three in a Bed

The next day, Manson, Brunner, and Fromme drove north into the redwood forests, where they rented a cabin on Brunner's dime. They slept awkwardly in the same bed, with Manson naked, Brunner in her underwear, and Fromme fully frocked in her peasant dress. Manson took them in his arms. "Neither of you know how perfect you are," he said, according to Fromme. She added: "I wanted to believe him but hid the thought quickly so as not to be taken for a fool. Nobody else had ever said that to me before."

The threesome was soon consummated. Fromme described it:

Charlie made love to me naturally—unlike the movies about moral frustration and the sudden manic-depressive mashing of mouths. He took his time. When I allowed it, he moved me.

*When I stopped it, he freed that energy, allowing me to feel
beyond anything I had experienced . . .*

　　*Charlie would make love to each of us and to both of us. He
once asked us each to sit in a chair and watch him make love to
the other. Beyond initial discomfort, I saw moving artwork and
dance, tenderness and surrender . . .*

　　*Intimacy between the three of us seemed illicit at first,
my mind constructing questions as barriers. Yet I could create
nothing that didn't dissolve in reality. Our skin felt natural,
our lips felt natural, and he felt natural between us. He moved
us so that we didn't need to think about it—sensually, rather
than with design—and we learned to relax into him. He
wondered if Mary and I were sexually attracted to each other . . .
But Mary and I were not bisexual. We were mutually sexually
attracted to him.*

Male Followers

Fromme summarized his appeal: "Charlie let us be beautiful."
Over the ensuing two years, he assembled a fluid-membership
harem of 25 or more women. He said they were there for the
taking: "These are your children. You threw them out, and I took
them in." And it wasn't only women who were beguiled. One
of Manson's key male followers, Charles Watson, known to the
Family as Tex, described him as a mystical shape-shifter: "Rock
star, guru, devil, son of God, even a child. He was a magician and
a charmer. He was aware, almost catlike. His eyes were hypnotic,
having the ability to psyche you out immediately."

Watson would become Manson's chief henchman, committing multiple murders at his direction. How did he enlist so many willing subjugates? As Dr. Raj Persaud and Dr. Peter Bruggen wrote in *Psychology Today*: "Manson has stood out as being of particular psychological fascination and revulsion because of his alleged ability to exercise such a mental hold over others, getting them to perform brutal slayings under his influence."

Paul Watkins, the musician—one of a handful of men allowed in Manson's inner circle (and, to me, one of the most astute analysts)—says that to understand the Family's bloody final destination you must first understand the path they took to get there. As he wrote in his memoir:

> *The public has always known Charles Manson as a murderer. They did not meet him, as I did, on that evening in March 1968 in Topanga Canyon. When I met him, there was no violence in the Family, no talk of Helter Skelter; in fact, it was the complete opposite. Charlie's love then was real. It had some integrity. But the public met Charlie through the media only after the murders; by then, the whole story was tainted with blood. To understand Charles Manson and the Family you have to see how they evolved, you have to make that journey as I did, from one end of the spectrum to the other.*

Ability to Spin Words

Many of his followers said Manson had an enthralling presence—despite his lack of physical stature—that was enhanced by his ability to spin words. Watkins included a passage in his memoir that gives a sense of Manson's preaching style:

> *It's like the man, dig . . . always programming us all the time . . . like society . . . programming us with all the garbage on TV: to wear certain clothes and eat certain foods, dig . . . to buy and produce all the rot that pollutes the earth . . . You see it all the time in the war . . . You see eighteen year old kids . . . and all the young love . . . programmed to be Marines . . . to hate gooks or Japs and to kill them with a bayonet in the name of democracy or the flag or whatever . . . but they make it out to be heroic, like an all-American dude, a hero, dig . . . just killing.*
>
> *What I see . . . is the animals are smarter than the people. In jail I hardly ever saw animals around. But then I got out and see the coyotes and dogs and snakes, rabbits and cats and mules and the horses. And I see the animals and watch them. And that's where the love is. Most of the love is in the animals and in the people, man. And that's where my love is. I don't really have a philosophy . . . Like I don't have any thought in my mind hardly at all. It's all love.*

"'Intense' is the word that best described Charlie during these raps," Watkins wrote.

> *He seemed totally energized and focused. He exuded an electric, almost seething passion. His words were infused with feeling, as though they had been issued from a bubbling cauldron of soul. When he spoke of love you felt warmth to your core. When he*

sang, his words were even more compelling . . . There was a beauty in his face, a bold, confident directness. There was also subtlety and cunning—a lupine glint in his eyes—the look of the wolf, the jackal; the soul of the scorpion.

Manson's Cornerstones

I'm pretty sure that prison savvy framed his cons more than any "lupine glint." He also fell into good fortune by quickly hooking up with Mary Brunner and Lynette Fromme, who became the cornerstones of Manson's ability to build a following. Fromme, a cute, clever, approachable little hippie chick, was Manson's favorite, who functioned as a leader of the followers. And Brunner, with her Midwestern manner, was the yin to Fromme's yang.

Fromme wrote of Brunner: "She might have been called taciturn, tough—at worst, abrupt, stub-jawed, button-lipped, and close-minded—but never for long. She was bright and attractive, her will was good, and she didn't bother with grudges. Charlie leaned on her for any necessary business and often said she had a lot of love."

These two appealing figures, the *prima* and *segundogénita* of Manson's Family, gave him credibility with other women. *Hey, if these two are on board, how bad can it be?* Brunner was the group's plodder, its accountant, and Fromme was more the frontwoman of the band, banging her tambourine for Charlie.

A Cult Leader's Qualities

For many of his followers, Manson was alluring because he represented danger. His status as a recent prison parolee gave him a cool factor. It was often the first biographical detail that his women used to describe him—perhaps it was an indicator of something known to psychologists as "hybristophilia," a fetish-like condition that causes women to be sexually stimulated by dangerous men.

In 1941, Hervey Milton Cleckley, a pioneering American psychiatrist, published a checklist of psychopathic traits in his book *The Mask of Sanity*. (He found fame in the 1950s when his case study of a patient with what was then known as multiple personality disorder became the subject of a book and a film, *The Three Faces of Eve*.) His list:

> *Superficial charm; considerable intelligence; absence of delusions; a lack of neurosis, considerable poise, and an ability to speak lucidly; a lack of responsibility and disregard for obligations; untruthfulness and insincerity; antisocial and impulsive behavior; poor judgment and failure to learn from experience; pathological egocentricity, including complete self-centeredness and an incapacity for genuine love, attachment, and deep emotions; lack of self-insight; ingratitude; objectionable behavior, including vulgarity, rudeness, mood swings, and silly pranks; impersonal sexual relations; and a failure to create a life plan—unless it is for destructive purposes or a sham.*

The criminal psychologist Robert Hare, Cleckley's colleague and collaborator, later expanded on that list to include such things as grandiosity, pathological lying, manipulative behavior, lack of remorse, a parasitic lifestyle, and sexual promiscuity. His checklist seemed to be a psychological profile of Manson:

The tendency to be smooth, engaging, charming, slick, and verbally facile . . . A psychopath never gets tongue-tied. He can also be a great listener, to simulate empathy while zeroing in on his targets' dreams and vulnerabilities, to be able to manipulate them better . . . A grossly inflated view of one's abilities and self-worth, self-assured, opinionated, cocky, a braggart. Psychopaths are arrogant people who believe they are superior human beings . . . Shrewd, crafty, cunning, sly, and clever . . . Deceptive, deceitful, underhanded, unscrupulous, manipulative and dishonest . . . A lack of feelings or concern for the losses, pain, and suffering of victims . . . Dispassionate, coldhearted . . . A disdain for one's victims . . . Emotional poverty or a limited range or depth of feelings; interpersonal coldness in spite of signs of open gregariousness and superficial warmth . . . An intentional, manipulative, selfish, and exploitative financial dependence on others . . . A variety of brief, superficial relations, numerous affairs, and an indiscriminate selection of sexual partners; the maintenance of numerous, multiple relationships at the same time; a history of attempts to sexually coerce others into sexual activity . . .

Master Manipulator

Manson was all that and more. He became a master manipulator of the vulnerable by using a prison survival technique: Tell them what they want to hear. First of all he intuited susceptibilities, and then he plastered over these yearnings with praise, encouragement, and gobbledygook that presaged New Age faux mysticism:

"I love all and all is me, but if there is no me, I love nothing."
He pasted together a *trompe l'oeil* of such nonsense, much of it
borrowed from Dale Carnegie books, Scientology pamphlets,
and other materials that passed through his hands in prison. For
his floundering followers, he seemed to have all the answers. He
frequently suggested that he was a reincarnation of Jesus Christ,
coyly claiming that he had been crucified long ago. (He often
posed as though hanging from a cross.) It probably didn't hurt
that his gullible followers were often high on narcotics, underfed,
or suffering a sex hangover.

Manson, who turned 33 in November 1967, was
significantly older than all of the women who followed him.
Some regard him as a predator, and he did have sex with
vulnerable teenagers as young as 14. But in most cases the prey
came to him—and were so enamored that they seemed not to
realize they were being consumed. In that sense, he was the
perfect manipulator for his times.

"His manipulative capacity was so advanced that Manson
was able to convince others to kill for him, which in most
historical and geographical settings would be unrealistic,"
writes Robin Altman, a scholar who analyzed Manson for a
University of Colorado honors thesis. "However, Manson
reached his full development in a time and place that provided
the perfect hunting ground for an unorganized but determined
psychopath: California in the 1960s."

The Vulnerability Factor

Contributing factors included a handful of the counterculture's
rebellious values: freedom from personal responsibility,

encouragement of casual sexual exploration, widespread recreational drug use, and weakened or broken ties with families and traditional roots organizations, such as churches.

A vivid illustration came in a letter that Patricia Krenwinkel, another of the earliest acolytes, sent from prison in 1970, after she had been charged with committing murder for Manson. Facing capital punishment, her lyrical account of life with Charlie showed that she was still drunk on the Manson Family Kool-Aid:

> *A time ago, but then it is always now, a disenchanted and frightened girl wandered aimlessly upon the sands of the Pacific shore, her mind filled with doubts and cares, knowing all is meaningless except the love of one another, but unwilling to extend her heart for fear of rejection. She might have ended as she had planned so often, a body swept upon the shore by the tide.*
>
> *'Twas but a smile, a true smile, one which you could touch with the warmth of your heart, and a glance—not like many you take, but one where you travel between two pairs of eyes, meet in the middle and know there is no beginning or end—a sudden load laid from your shoulders and a sureness of your faith—and to your own surprise you find someone who understands your every thought, a friend, ah, much more, a reflection of yourself, the hidden beauty that you find openly in another face looking into your own.*
>
> *It was then, in that strange stillness of unspeakable aloneness and togetherness, that brought me here to now. 'Twas but a few days before Charlie, Mary, Lyn, and I began traveling the roads in a cozy VW bus, exchanging thoughts composed of*

all our fears, sorrows and loves, making of each other a family, strong by the bonds of understanding, experience of the road filling the longing of wants and making of us all one spirit of joy and laughter. For as long as you are together with each other, there is no moment of despair.

Note Krenwinkel's allusion to suicide. She was one of several of Manson's acolytes who found Manson amid depression, including Susan Atkins. After belatedly rejecting Manson, Atkins wrote about his supposed mystical manipulations of troubled young women:

Considerable media attention has been given to Charles Manson's ability to "control the minds of his followers." His ability to "brainwash" people. "Hypnotize." "Zombyize." But if you look at his methods of controlling people you will see no mystic clairvoyance, no unearthly super-power. What you will see is that he knows no more about "brainwashing" than any other pimp in Los Angeles.

He took young people, primarily girls, who had poor family relations, low self-esteem, and who felt they didn't belong. He took them away from their familiar surroundings. He took them to an isolated place where he could control what they saw, heard, and learned. He prevented them from making attachments outside his group. He took away all their money under the pretext that the Family would provide for them—which not only prevented them from leaving but also made them dependent on him even for their clothes, food, and shelter. He sowed dissension and bitterness toward outsiders. He encouraged them to become

*dependent on drugs—drugs which he alone would disperse. And
then, to polish it all off, he threw in a sizable portion of brutal
physical abuse.*

Nineteenth-Century Forerunners

Manson is often portrayed as an aberration—a parasitic immoral
rogue who took advantage of nonplussed young women cast into
the tempestuous high seas of the sexual revolution. In fact, he
was a link in a long chain of male manipulators, before and after.
His antecedents include the persuasive men who for centuries
have built followings that often center on the leader's access to
multiple sexual partners. Joseph Smith, who founded the Mormon
faith in 1830, had 40 wives, including some adolescents, and his
successor, Brigham Young, topped Smith with 55.

In many ways the 1800s were a harbinger of the free-love
Sixties, as the perfectionist movement prompted the creation
of more than three dozen utopia-seeking communal groups
in the U.S. alone. One sex-centered example was the Oneida
Community, founded in 1848 in upstate New York by Vermont
native John Humphrey Noyes. The group practiced what Noyes
characterized as "complex marriage." Schedule ledgers allowed
members to make appointments for assignations, although Noyes
had dibs as "first husband"—all for the glory of God.

As Spencer Klaw wrote in his book examining the
commune: "Girls were ordinarily introduced to sex, usually by
Noyes himself, as soon as they reached puberty." Klaw added:
"Noyes was a man of powerful sexual drives, and for many years
he was perhaps the most active participant in the sexual life of the

Brigham Young, a persuasive man, who built a following that centered on its leader's access to multiple sexual partners.

community. He was a connoisseur of female sexuality."

A letter from a young female member named Beulah Hendee offers an insight into Noyes' sexual magnetism. Hendee joined the commune in 1864, at age 17, and shortly thereafter offered her body to the boss. She described her first romp with Noyes with the same sort of mysticism that Manson's followers used when they framed their first sexual encounters with him. Hendee wrote: "I went to his room and told him I could do one thing, and that was to submit myself to him and look for his spirit to enter into me and fill me. I . . . sat down by him and unburdened myself. He is so full of mercy and tenderness."

John Humphrey Noyes, who announced his "sinless perfection" in 1834, was arrested for his views on free love in 1846, and founded the Oneida Community in 1848.

After 31 years (and nine children with nearly as many women), Noyes abandoned the commune and fled to Canada in 1879 after he was tipped off to his impending arrest for statutory rape, on the grounds of carnal knowledge with juveniles. He lived out his life in exile, although his remains were interred in the commune cemetery after he died in 1886.

Post-Manson Cults

Many other U.S. cults landed on the front pages after the Manson Family. During the 1970s, the country puzzled over an amorphous, California-based group known by various names: The Family International, Teens for Christ, The Children of God, and The Family of Love. It was an insular, apocalyptic group that won the sex-cult crown in 1976, by using a form of evangelism it called "Flirty Fishing" to "show God's love and mercy"—and lure male recruits. In brief, female members prostituted themselves in "deep witness" to the cause.

November 1978 brought the shocking mass suicide of more than 900 followers of kooky Jim Jones, who had predicted a nuclear apocalypse. The deaths occurred in Guyana in South America, where Jones established a colony for his People's Temple after he was run out of California. Jones forbade sex between unmarried members, but treated himself to liaisons with both male and female followers.

The early 1990s cast attention on David Koresh, leader of a heavily armed Seventh-Day Adventist faction that holed up in a compound near Waco, Texas, to wait out Armageddon. Koresh had several things in common with Manson: both were semi-literate school dropouts who played guitar and harbored dashed dreams of rock 'n' roll stardom, and like Manson Koresh had a voracious sexual thirst that he quenched freely and frequently with his acolytes, some reportedly as young as ten years old. Koresh and 75 of his followers died in a controversial federal raid on his compound in 1993.

One of the most far-out cult self-destructions came in March 1997, when 39 men and women took part in a carefully orchestrated mass suicide at a rented villa near San Diego, California. Each body was laid out in bed clad in black sweatpants, a black button-down tunic and out-of-the-box Nike jogging shoes, and every torso and shorn head was enshrouded by a square of deep-purple fabric. All wore a Star Trek-inspired arm patch that read: "Heaven's Gate Away Team," and computers in the mansion flashed a Starship Enterprise-style "Red Alert."

The Heaven's Gate cult left video manifestos explaining that disciples were "exiting their human vessels" and beaming up to what they believed was an extraterrestrial-piloted spaceship zipping along in the blue ion tail of the comet Hale–Bopp, a bright light in the night sky for more than a year.

"The little people I had been looking for had come to take me home," said one young man in a video he left behind.

The plan was inspired by the cult's leader, a bug-eyed wackadoodle from west Texas named Marshall Applewhite. He began fancying himself a prophet in the midst of a nervous breakdown prompted by a sexual identity crisis in the 1970s. Twenty-five years later, he led acolytes into the wild blue yonder of their minds (with an overdose of phenobarbital), where they expected to ride to the "kingdom level above human" in the comfort of a UFO. I'm not sure that particular detail worked out.

Cultists' Mind-Control Tactics

How do so many patently mad cultists find so many willing followers?

As Manson was being released from prison in 1967, an important new academic book was introducing American sociologists to the mind-control tactics of an emerging fringe faith—the "Moonies" of the Unification Church. Its founder, Sun Myung Moon, was a wealthy South Korean businessman who claimed to be a messiah. He had begun by sending Asian emissaries to college campuses to recruit members. John Lofland, a doctoral candidate in sociology at Cal-Berkeley, conducted research on the Moonies for his thesis, which was published as a book in 1966. Its title gave a brand to that era's end-time preppers: *Doomsday Cult: A Study of Conversion, Proselytization, and Maintenance of Faith*. Lofland and other experts have delineated the steps through which Moonies and other cults lure their faithful. They include:

- *Seek out and recruit vulnerable people and use converts to recruit more converts.*
- *Induce dependency by stripping recruits of assets so they rely on the group for food, clothing, and shelter.*
- *Isolate them from outside influences, particularly loved ones, who are renounced and blamed for the recruit's personal failings.*
- *Envelop members in tranquilizing messages of peace, love, and happiness.*
- *Engage members in emotional, romantic, or sexual relationships that bind individuals to the group.*
- *Present the leader as the embodiment of a messenger from God who holds the key to eternal life.*
- *Groom members to accept the leader's clairvoyance and other special powers.*
- *Ostracize and shame nonbelievers.*
- *Introduce forewarnings of a coming apocalyptic event that will mean death for most and survival for only select believers.*
- *Begin preparations to survive, including food storage and weapons stockpiling.*

Whether through research or instinct, Manson employed each of these methods. And although his Family may not have been conceived as a doomsday cult, the group ticked all the boxes by the end, as it prepped to ride out an apocalyptic "Helter Skelter" race war in the Death Valley desert with their self-styled Christ reincarnate.

What Do They Think Now?

To this day, a handful of his acolytes continue to cling to the belief that Manson was a misunderstood benevolent prophet. Lynette Fromme's memoir is a myopic affirmation of her life with Manson. In her telling, the murders—mentioned only tangentially—were irrelevant to the wonders of life with Charlie. I understand her position. To renounce Manson now would be to admit that she had spent her entire adult life in an illusion. Who wants to admit that they fell for a smooth-talking jailbird's 50-year con job?

Dianne Lake, barely a teenager when she joined the Family, quickly renounced Manson after the murders and slipped into a self-imposed obscurity while she regained her footing and, eventually, raised a family. In her 2017 memoir, she tried to explain how she had fallen under Manson's thrall:

> *There is no doubt that Charlie took advantage of me. This small man oozed self-confidence and sex appeal, and as he would demonstrate time and time again in the months and years ahead, he knew exactly what he was doing. He was a master manipulator, while I was fourteen and essentially on my own. I was a naïve, lonely, love-starved little girl looking for a parental*

figure to tell me, "No, don't do that." . . . When he focused his attention on you, he made you believe there was no one else in the world. He also had the uncanny sensibility bestowed upon mystics, yet misused by sociopaths and con men, to know exactly what you need. Charlie knew what you were afraid of . . . But perhaps the most impressive trick of all was how he made this seem as if it was my idea.

Before her renouncement, the highly sexualized Lake was regarded with distaste by some of her female commune-mates. Her 24-hour comeliness cast her as the Family's own Valeria Messalina, the Roman emperor's wife who has gone down in history as the woman who couldn't get enough.

CHAPTER FOUR

Who's Charlie With?

late in 1967, the Manson Family was flopping at a tumbledown house near the bottom of Topanga Canyon, just across the Pacific Highway from the deep-blue sea, at the point where two of the region's most gilded addresses, Malibu and Pacific Palisades, converge. The hilltop villa museum of oil tycoon J. Paul Getty was a short hike away. Somebody had carelessly built the two-story house in the floodplain of Topanga Creek, and intermittent high water tumbling down the canyon had rendered it uninhabitable—for anyone with common sense. After the owner had abandoned the house, it became a wide-open temporary hideaway for transient hippies, bikers, grifters, and miscellaneous miscreants. The Manson clan simply parked its black school bus outside and took up residence over the course of several months. Although the ground floor was ankle-deep in sand, the silt-free upper level was accessible via the structure's most striking feature, exterior circular steps that gave the house its hippie nickname: the Spiral Staircase. For reasons that none of the floppers could quite fathom, the house had functioning plumbing, water, and electricity. Author Nuel Emmons described the place:

To those who live within society's moral code, the house might have resembled a movie scene of a massive party at a dope fiend's pad: music playing, often blaring, sometimes soft and sensual; strobe lights blinking, or hardly any light at all; guys and girls everywhere, seated on couches, chairs and pillows, on the floors and on the beds; marijuana joints passed around; tables showing long lines of coke; pills and capsules of all colors, each providing a different high; long-haired, bearded guys in weird clothes with

exaggerated lengths of gold and beaded chains; scantily-clad girls,
obviously drugged, willing to have sex . . .

Communal Revival

If you live an orthodox life today, it might be difficult to reckon why so many young people aspired to the hippie lifestyle. Yet the Manson Family was far from unusual. Hundreds of communes were founded in California alone, due in part to its welcoming climate. But a communal revival was happening everywhere in the U.S.—and far beyond in parts of Europe, notably including Great Britain and Denmark.

Mortified by frightening contemporary trends such as race riots and choking pollution, some people were looking for a better way to live, somehow closer to the earth, at arm's length from the disturbing events over which they had no control. Communes were popping up like mushrooms after a rainstorm in the East Village of New York City, in the Catskill Mountains to the north, in New England, and in cities large and small, coast to coast. Consider the regional counterculture metrics for southern California alone. Greater Los Angeles had a population of 10 million in 1970. If just one out of a thousand wished to get back to the earth, a hippie legion of 10,000 would have ascended into the hills, seeking a smaller life, a larger truth—and a place to flop, like the Spiral Staircase.

Snake's Arrival

One evening, Manson and his women were in the midst of a frequent ritual there, sitting cross-legged in a circle as Charlie cradled his guitar and led them in a singalong. Suddenly, the door squeaked open, and in walked a teenager who had been invited by a friend. It was Dianne Lake, who was 14 years old. The Family was expecting her.

"Dianne is here! Dianne is here!" Lynette Fromme exclaimed. "You're even prettier than your picture! Charlie is going to be so happy to meet you!"

Police mugshot of Dianne Lake. Dianne was a free-range adolescent, whose arrival upset the Family apple cart.

Lake was a free-range adolescent who had been released into the urban L.A. wild by hippie parents who were fixtures at Wavy Gravy's Hog Farm commune, over the mountains in the San Fernando Valley. She had been run off the farm because she was having sex with adults, and Wavy Gravy feared criminal consequences. By coincidence, Manson's group had become acquainted with Lake's parents through commune circles, and the child's mother had shown them a photo of Dianne, in the hope that Fromme and the others would keep an eye on her should their paths cross. So Fromme instantly recognized her when she walked up the spiral staircase and into the Manson Family as its youngest member.

Among the Family's females, Lake has long been an object of particular fascination because of her age. Known by the slithering nickname "Snake," she has been characterized by some other members of the cult as a clueless stoner and an oversexed vixen who upset a delicate balance in the crowded competition for access to Charlie's reproductive hardware. Sandra Good, like Fromme a lifelong devotee to Manson, tried to explain the complicated dance in a letter from prison during the 1970s. She wrote:

The dynamics between Charlie and each person were as numerous as the people and changed hour by hour. Often, he was a blur to me because he was always moving, always going somewhere with someone, or lying down with a girl. I could torture myself wondering who he was with, and I saw others, particularly Bo [Rosenberg] *and Snake, hovering and inquiring, "Where's Charlie? Who is he with?"*

Good had a particular issue with Lake, despite her underage status. She believed Lake crossed a line by being too forward in trying to lure Manson to her honey. Good wrote:

Snake was in a category by herself, the youngest of us and most eccentric . . . Her eyes were often at half-mast whether due to the weed she liked so much or to what looked to me to be near constant sexual arousal. It was by seeing her lip-licking attempts to draw Charles that I learned that raw sex was not what attracted him. Snake had been weaned too young from a straight world to a hippie world . . . She had her sixteen-year-old libido [fourteen, in fact] *and few social skills to navigate amongst more worldly people.*

In her 2017 memoir, Lake recounted her first encounter with Manson at the Spiral Staircase:

Charlie stood up and looked into my eyes so deeply and intimately that I almost turned away on instinct. Instead I held his gaze and felt like he was looking into me.

"So, this is our Dianne," he said and pulled me to his chest in a hug so close I could feel his heartbeat. He held on for several seconds and I felt my resistance fade. I was used to the hippie hugs at the Hog Farm, but this felt warm and real. Tears welled up into my eyes as I took in his embrace.

Charlie held me at arm's length, looked at me and said, "Oh, you're beautiful. I want to talk to you. I've been looking for you."

Ritual Newcomer Sex

Lake said she was invited into the song circle—directly at Manson's side—and immediately fell under his trance. She described him as "charming, witty, and most of all intriguing." As the night wore on, it was clear that everyone in the room understood that Lake was bound for ritual newcomer sex. Lynette Fromme and Patricia Krenwinkel, both exalted acolytes, caressed and cooed over Lake, directing blunts of weed to her lips, like elder courtesans grooming an initiate for the sultan. Finally, Manson raised an eyebrow and set aside his guitar. Lake described what happened next:

He stood, took my hand, and led me outside. We walked hand in hand to the black bus. He went in first and motioned for me to follow. It reminded me of a raja's palace, with mattresses on the floor and Indian-print bedspreads and carpets hanging from the walls. Pillows were strewn about and colorful swirls were painted on any surface not already covered with fabric. . . . We sat facing each other and the anticipation swelled up inside me. I expected a kiss, but instead Charlie had me put my hands up against his. He moved his hands in different directions until I caught on that I was to follow his every move. It was a game, and I was more than eager to play. It was like he was syncing up our energy. He sped up until I could no longer follow, and he started to laugh. Then he guided me onto the mattress and again looked into my eyes so that I felt there was no one else but the two of us in the entire world. "You are so beautiful, my little one." His voice was barely above a whisper, but I heard it reverberate through my consciousness.

We had only smoked pot, but I felt as if I were on a trip, his trip, and he was guiding my every move. Charlie was older than the other men I had slept with, but his body seemed younger. He had tattoos on his arms and a small tuft of hair on his chest. There was something magnetic about him, even though I wasn't sure I even found him attractive. He was small and nice-looking but not as classically handsome as some of the men I had pursued. The attraction was more chemical and inevitable without any thought about whether I would or wouldn't.

He took his time to explore my body. He avoided the places that made me purr until I could barely stand it. After a few minutes, he put himself inside me while staring into my eyes. He was tender as he held me up to meet his deep thrusts. When he finished, he sighed; I exhaled and realized I was hooked . . . My experience with Charlie was the beginning of something. I felt appreciated by him, not just like some pretty young thing. Charlie was offering me more than sex . . . He said everything I needed to hear.

Lake found her happy place with the Manson Family—a place where "Charlie and the girls made it OK for me to want and have sex." She said in 2017: "[Manson] made you feel like you were his one and only love. Yes, there were other girls, but we all shared him. He made you feel really special, and specially loved."

Cosmic Orgasm

But life in the Family was not all rainbows, unicorns, and orgasms. There was only so much of little Charlie's penis to go around—and that led to resentment and back-biting by the have-nots. The whereabouts of Manson's manhood became an increasingly complicated question as membership grew. Sandra Good griped in a letter from behind bars about "my constant frustration with the arrival of new girls." She said:

Charlie obviously loved making love to pretty women. Although anything of beauty caught his eye, all of nature was beautiful to him, and I learned that women who were most comfortable being close to nature, who didn't wear make-up or try to look like magazine covers, appealed to him more than what he once called "plastic fantastics."

Manson invited his small cadre of male followers to share the load. Fromme said he "always encouraged us girls to give the young guys a chance, not just for sexual experience, but for the natural human interactions that allow boys to become men." She wrote: "Half a dozen women always awaited Charlie's touch, and every so often he took his time, laying us out like delicacies to be savored. He was also genuinely instructive to the younger guys." She described an orgy where "all of us lay naked on the white rugs beside the fire." Manson observed the foreplay between two teenage family members, Nancy Pitman and Paul Watkins, the resident stoner. Watkins seemed rather wooden in rubbing his lover's leg, so Manson pressed his hand on Watkins' and said: "Easy. This isn't a piece of furniture. It's a work of art."

Manson had broad sexual tastes—both male and female.

"Certainly, Charlie's sexual appetites, though erratic, were voracious," Paul Watkins wrote in his 1979 memoir, *My Life with Charles Manson*. He was obsessed with staging a "cosmic orgasm" during group sex, which Manson said would allow the family to pass through "the last door" of self-actualization. Watkins recounted one such attempt in the fall of 1968, which commenced after Manson—bare-chested and dressed in buckskin leggings—gave a hash-inspired speech that ended in the phrase: "It's all love." According to Watkins, the group sex would begin after Manson "gave out a gut-wrenching yowl, and immediately the others began shouting, moaning and screaming, giving vent to a cacophony of noise . . . though I was initially startled by the raucous outburst, I immediately understood it as a kind of tension release, a collective purging of the soul." Here is his description of the Family's mass love-making, featuring six men and 14 women:

We went through the preliminaries of joining hands and making sounds, but most of it was unnecessary. Everyone seemed tuned in. Generally, just one person's uptightness was enough to throw discord into a scene, but not that night. The vibes were right. It was all the more unusual, since we had two new girls in the Family, Ouisch [Ruth Ann Moorehouse, then just 17] *and* Gypsy [Catherine Share].

Before long I was lying on my back with Snake on my left. I had my hand on her thigh while Stephanie lay on my right with one of her legs draped over mine. Stephanie Rowe was another girl I grew very fond of. She was quick-witted and capable, and at times would engage in friendly verbal fencing matches with Charlie. She had dark strong features and thick brown hair. A slight tendency to corpulence inhibited her on occasion, but for the most part she was very much on top of the scene. She'd been with Charlie since the San Francisco days, and was a passionate lover. She smelled clean and fragrant that night as she rolled over and put her arm around my waist, while Ella [Bailey] *moved over from the left and began giving head to Snake.*

Since there were always fewer men, the women prepared each other by initiating foreplay—readying themselves for the men, who would subsequently move from girl to girl while trying to maintain the rhythm of the group. I was aware of the breathing in the room. It sounded like an organism, as if I was connected respiratorily to everyone. The fire was still crackling, spewing up smoke through the flue. The back windows were open so that fresh air circulated like some invisible external aphrodisiac moving in a rhythm with the breathing and the languorous sounds of the lovemakers.

I don't know if the whole Family was in tune with the little scene that five or six of us had going, but I do know that at no previous time had I experienced such a free, natural flow of movement. I had complete control as I moved from one girl to the next. It seemed as if I was penetrating all of them simultaneously and that we were all in tune—an alchemy of human juices mingling and swirling in orifices belonging to us all. There was no hesitation, no holding back . . .

Much later that night, Charlie came over with a new girl named Darcy. I was aware of them lying beside me. Almost everyone else was sleeping—a sea of bodies . . . It was dark except for a candle burning on the windowsill . . . Charlie asked her if she felt the cosmic vibes that night. She said yes. Then he said sex was just an expression of love: "If you love, you just love . . . physical and spiritual love are one love." Then he told her to give him some head. When she went down on him he stopped her. "Hey, no, no, not like that . . . Paul can do better than that. Hey, Paul . . . show this girl how to give head, will ya." Charlie was testing me, and I knew it. The thought repulsed me as I looked at him and then at the girl. But I was starting to believe in Charlie. I wanted to please him so I showed her. "Freedom," Charlie said later, "is a turn-on to cosmic law, and in cosmic law there is no gender, it's just love."

Rivalry Between Followers

Lynette Fromme was envied by many of the others for her special status in Manson's bed, and he did not share her often with other males. (Paul Watkins said he never understood Fromme's vaunted position with Manson "until many months later, when I made love to her the first time.") Vincent Bugliosi, Manson's prosecutor and biographer, said everyone in the Family understood that Fromme was Manson's favorite. Sandra Good, who couldn't get enough of Manson, certainly noticed. As she wrote about Fromme in a letter from prison: "I was envious of her position and her sheer luck in meeting him nearly a year before I did and having only a few other women around instead of over ten."

Fromme and Good would eventually bond as Manson's forever-girls, staying faithful to their fantasy long after everyone else had returned to reality. Fromme described her kindred spirit in her memoir:

Sandra Good was like the faceless secretary in old movies who becomes stunning with the simple removal of hairpins and glasses. In real life, she clung to her reservations, and seemed to want to observe the rest of us rather than participate in what we were doing. At times she was so removed as not to be seen.

Good was unsparing in criticisms of her competition. Here is what she had to say about Susan Atkins, nicknamed Sadie: "Sadie was the only person I didn't like. She was arrogant, bossy, and condescending towards many of us. And she was man-hungry and didn't seem clean." She got the blame for any outbreak of sexually transmitted disease in the Family—and there were many. Fromme included in her memoir this scathing little poem she penned about Atkins:

Cocky Sadie, gallivantin' lady, see how she strut!
Always on the heel and toe, always putting on a show,
The smaller the pants, the bigger the butt.
O, Sadie, Sadie Mae, who did you fall in love with today?
Will you tell us, or are you going away?
Sittin' cross-legged in your black silk scanties
Evilest of all their aunties, bragged bold and bare-faced,
Getting your high-heeled boots laced . . .

How the Group Got Started

Manson chose to grin rather than engage in these sexual tiffs, but a couple of his comments in the vast Manson archive showed his sexual interest to be more carnal than mystical. Asked by a female TV reporter in the late 1990s about his grip on women, he growled: "I fuck real good." But his most telling explanation of how in the world a failed criminal and former pimp with no prospects managed to lure so many young women came in an interview with *Life* magazine in 1987. It was another moment when he acknowledged his con. He was asked by a journalist: "How did this group get started?" His reply:

> *I get out of the penitentiary—a man can understand this—and*
> *I haven't been with a broad in a long time. So I meet a broad on*
> *the street corner. She's real young. So I ask to stay with this other*
> *broad* [Mary Brunner]. *So we meet another chick* [that] *didn't*
> *have no place to stay. That was Squeaky* [Lynette Fromme].
> *Then we meet Patty* [Krenwinkel]— *and Patty's got a credit*

card! So we're just going to have a little vacation trip, so we get a bus. We're just tripping. And Susie [Atkins] wants to freeload, see? So I look up and I'm sitting on the beach with 12 girls. They're lighting my cigarettes, spoiling me, and actually it's a pretty nice little trip I've got going.

CHAPTER FIVE

Good Vibrations

In 1968 the Beach Boys were in the midst of an existential crisis. The surfer-boy shtick—the band's hit-making "formula" that brought great riches to its young members—had worn thin on Brian Wilson, the fragile genius who was the band's creative pivot man. On the one hand, how could a southern California band whose very name evoked sunshine and sandy butts shift to cranking out the edgy new psychedelic sounds of San Francisco's Jefferson Airplane or the Grateful Dead? On the other, the Beach Boys were at risk of becoming an oldies act, just six years after catching their first wave in 1962 with "Surfin' Safari." It had been two years since their last big hit, "Good Vibrations." A depressed Brian Wilson had begun to retreat to his bedroom, and three consecutive LPs had fallen flat, dating to his 1966 artistic masterpiece, *Pet Sounds*. The boys left behind—his brothers Carl and Dennis Wilson, Al Jardine, and front man Mike Love, who advocated the old formulaic surf rock—were desperate for fresh material.

Fateful Encounter

In March 1968, drummer Dennis Wilson was cruising Los Angeles in his Rolls-Royce when he stopped for two young women hitchhikers. He gave them a lift to their destination and went on his way—no big deal—but it seemed more like destiny than chance when he found the same two women, Patricia Krenwinkel and Ella Jo Bailey, both members of the Manson Family, thumbing a ride a few months later in Malibu. This time, he took them home to the 20-room mountain lodge-style mansion—complete with peacocks roaming the grounds—that he was renting in Pacific Palisades.

Carl and Dennis Wilson (right) on a visit to London in 1968. Dennis was cruising Los Angeles in his Rolls-Royce when he stopped to pick up Patricia Krenwinkel and Ella Jo Bailey. He invited them to his Pacific Palisades home.

Dennis, two years older than Carl and two years younger than Brian, was the band's fast-living heart-throb, with a leading man's chin and an insatiable appetite for hot rods, women, and intoxicants. Famously, the athletic Dennis was also the only member of the band who could actually hang ten on a surfboard. Friends said Wilson had a silly, sweet boyishness and a childlike openness—or naivety—that persisted throughout what would be an abbreviated life. Perhaps he was frozen in time, because he was just 16 years old when he banged out the backbeat for the band's first single, "Surfin'," recorded in October 1961. With his wallet suddenly bulging, he did what most nouveau riche teenagers would do.

"He was buying things," explained Hal Blaine, the studio drummer from L.A.'s Wrecking Crew who played on many Beach Boys hits. "When you're sixteen years old and you're literally handed millions of dollars, you get crazy."

One of those crazy things, as Dennis Wilson would learn in retrospect, was his bizarre association with the Manson Family, one of the most intriguing mixes of popular music and murder since Stagger Lee shot Billy Lyons in a St. Louis barfight on Christmas Day 1895.

"You probably wouldn't have guessed that the Manson Family and the Beach Boys had a long history together," David Dalton wrote in *Rolling Stone*. "White racist Satan and the Doris Day of rock groups. But this is southern California, baby. Worlds collide. Surf boards and Sufis, kitsch and apocalypse, dune buggies and doomsday cults, live right next door to each other."

The Family Moves In

After Manson had gained notoriety, Wilson wouldn't reveal much about how the accused mass killer had managed to jimmy his way into the rock star's life. ("I'll never talk about that," he would say.) But he left one clear account, an interview conducted "over food and drinks" at the London Hilton in December 1968 by the British music journalist David Griffiths, while the band was in town recording a live album. Even then, eight months before the Tate and LaBianca murders, and a full year before Manson's arrest, Wilson felt qualms about speaking of his association. ("I don't know why I'm telling you all this," he told Griffiths.) He had good reason to be leery. The headline on the story, which appeared in the December 21, 1968, edition of the *Record Mirror*, a British music weekly, screamed:

DENNIS WILSON: "I LIVE WITH 17 GIRLS"

Griffiths' story explained that Wilson and his repeat-customer women hitchhikers had bonded over gurus. Through Mike Love, the band had become associated with Maharishi Mahesh Yogi, the Indian Transcendental Meditation master whose fans also included George Harrison of the Beatles. The hitchhikers, Krenwinkel and Bailey, said they had their own guiding light. "I told them about our involvement with the Maharishi," Wilson explained to the *Record Mirror*, "and they told me they too had a guru, a guy named Charlie who's recently come out of jail after 13 years." Of course, Guru Charlie was Charles Manson.

Wilson left the hitchhikers at his house and drove down into Los Angeles for a studio session. According to the lore—repeated so often by Manson biographers that it's almost certainly not true—Wilson and Manson first met when the drummer returned home at 3 a.m. and found his house full of women and their diminutive guru. The story goes that Wilson, sensing danger, asked Manson, "Are you going to hurt me?" and Manson is said to have responded by dropping to his knees and kissing Wilson's feet. For Wilson, it was brotherly love at first sight.

The interview in London offers a glimpse into Wilson's drug-addled mind during the months he hosted Manson—and the open acceptance of hallucinogens in his social circle. He mentioned psychedelic drugs several times, including in a wandering riff on the evolving musical sensibilities of the Beach Boys.

The public is evolving too. A couple of years ago, we got very paranoid about the possibility of losing our public. We were getting loaded, taking acid, and we made a whole album which we scrapped. Instead, we went to Hawaii, rested up, and then came out with the "Smiley Smiles" album, all new material. Drugs played a great role in our evolution but as a result we were frightened that people would no longer understand us, musically. We no longer feel that way. I know I am more in tune with my mind. I feel easier and more confident of myself . . .

Wilson said he was high on LSD the second time he picked up the women, whom he called "the space ladies." Griffiths asked whether Wilson was supporting his flock of birds. He replied: "No. If anything, they're supporting me. I had all the rich status symbols—Rolls-Royce, Ferrari, home after home. Then I woke up, gave away 50 to 60 percent of my money. Now I live in one small room with one candle, and I'm happy, finding myself."

Charles Manson was eager to help in that search.

Charlie's Rock Star Dream

Manson believed he deserved rock stardom, so imagine his glee at making the acquaintance of an A-list L.A. star with deep connections in the music industry. Although he was relatively new to the instrument, Manson was a decent guitarist who could sing in tune. Behind prison walls, he had taken guitar lessons from Alvin (Creepy) Karpis, of all people, an iconic American Depression-era gangster who became infamous as J. Edgar Hoover's Public Enemy No. 1 before his capture and imprisonment in 1936. In 1962, Karpis joined Manson at McNeil Island federal prison near Tacoma, Washington, when the feds closed Alcatraz, his home for 26 years. In his autobiography, Karpis explained the connection:

> *This kid approaches me to request music lessons. He wants to learn guitar and become a music star. "Little Charlie" is so lazy and shiftless, I doubt if he'll put in the time required to learn. The youngster has been in institutions all of his life— first orphanages, then reformatories, and finally federal prison. His mother, a prostitute, was never around to look after him. I decide it's time someone did something for him, and to my surprise, he learns quickly. He has a pleasant voice and a pleasing personality, although he's unusually meek and mild for a convict. He never has a harsh word to say and is never involved in even an argument.*

Karpis apparently taught him well, although Manson played an acoustic guitar with nylon strings, a folky sound in an era when the more biting tone of steel-string electric guitars was the way to play.

Enthralled by "the Wizard"

Despite his fame and wealth, Dennis Wilson was as needy and vulnerable as any of Manson's acolytes. And like many of them, he had a fractured relationship with his father, an abusive taskmaster. Dennis blew through five marriages in an abbreviated lifetime and used random sex, drugs, and alcohol to try to fill a void in his soul. He admired Manson, who reflected the counterculture cool in a way that the square Beach Boys never could. Wilson took to calling Manson "the Wizard," and he told friends that his new pal was both a god and a devil.

His bandmates were less enthused, especially Mike Love, who had a complicated relationship with all three of his Wilson cousins, although he was particularly spiteful and dismissive of Dennis.

"Dennis was enthralled by him," Mike Love said, "and it didn't hurt that Charlie Manson came with this group of girls." He added: "I only met the guy one time, and that was enough."

Skinny-Dippers and Orgies

But that was a memorable encounter, a dinner party he attended with Bruce Johnston, who had replaced Brian Wilson as a touring member of the band.

"Bruce Johnston and I were the only people at dinner who had clothing on," Love explained. "Everybody else was completely naked. So first of all, that's a little weird . . . Right after dinner, Charlie invited everybody to go in a den area, and turned on a strobe light, and passed out what was said to be acid, which I declined. I wasn't interested in doing that, nor was I interested in joining the bodies that were, you know, on the floor."

Love insisted that he did not partake of the orgy and went home unmolested to his wife and family, but the white rugs pitched on the living room floor in front of a big stone fireplace had seen their share of body fluids. The house was a legendary sex venue for the interlocking bodies of the Manson clan and assorted guests, often including Dennis Wilson and other figures from the music industry, with whom Manson sought to curry favor. Sometimes the orgies spilled over into Wilson's California-shaped swimming pool, where skinny-dippers bobbed day and night.

Wilson's libido often outflanked his common sense. Mike Love said Dennis was "the perfect mark" for "a stable of young women who catered to his every need." The Manson Family made itself at home, using Wilson's credit cards and his collection of expensive automobiles. They sometimes even drove the Rolls-Royce on dumpster-diving missions to grocery stores to retrieve discarded vegetables, bread, and sweets. Lynette Fromme said that while the other Beach Boys she met were inhospitable, she found Dennis Wilson to be charming and agreeable. "He was likeable and funny without trying to be, loose, whimsical, and with few reservations," she wrote. Wilson said he was "coming to consciousness" and whined that he wanted to go on the road with the Manson Family instead of the Beach Boys.

Sandra Good, Manson's patient lady-in-waiting, said long ago in a letter from prison that Wilson tried his best to claim her from Manson. She explained: "Dennis composed songs for me in his studio, and held me in his arms in his swimming pool, yet he held no charge or interest for me. Only Manson did, because he seemed to offer something that intimated peace, joy, and fulfillment."

Manson the Songwriter

Soon after they met, Manson played some of his original tunes for Dennis Wilson. "I found he had great musical ideas," Wilson said in the London interview. "We're writing together now. He's dumb, in some ways, but I accept his approach and have learned from him." The two men became fast music bros—and dance partners. "He taught me a dance, The Inhibition," Wilson said. "You have to imagine you're a frozen man and the ice is thawing out. Start with your fingertips, then all the rest of you, then you extend it to a feeling that the whole universe is thawing out . . ." Manson had a catalog of perhaps 15 original songs and many fragments. Their themes were consistent with his lifestyle. Female submission was a core lyrical concept, including in a jazzy tune entitled "Home Is Where You're Happy":

> *So burn all your bridges*
> *Leave your whole life behind*
> *You can do what you want to do*
> *'Cause you're strong in your mind.*

Another tune that urged compliance, "Cease to Exist," caught Wilson's ear. Its lyric included these lines:

> *Cease to exist/Come on and be with me . . .*
> *Just come and say you love me/Give up your world . . .*
> *Submission is a gift/Go on, give it to your brother.*

Wilson took the song into the studio, and the Beach Boys recorded it in the fall of 1968, with Dennis singing lead—and taking the writing credit. He retitled the song "Never Learn Not to Love" and tweaked the lyrics slightly; for example, the first line was changed to "cease to resist." The reworked song was included on their LP *20/20*, another relative flop released in February 1969. It was a mishmash of tunes—a meditative drone, reclaimed extras from earlier recording sessions, and strange covers, including Huddie Ledbetter's "Cotton Fields" and Ersel Hickey's rockabilly ballad, "Bluebirds Over the Mountain." Just two songs cracked the Top 25—a cover of "I Can Hear Music," a minor hit two years earlier for the Ronettes, and the original "Let's Do it Again," a surf-rock throwback. The Manson tune was also released on a single, the B-side to "Bluebirds Over the Mountain."

The Family Wears Out Its Welcome

But by the time the band performed Manson's song on *The Mike Douglas Show* that winter, his gang had worn out its welcome after three months of sex, drugs, and rock 'n' roll at Wilson's pad. And the bros had a falling out over the recording. Wilson claimed he paid Manson for the song with a motorcycle and a wad of cash and that Manson refused a writing credit. But the little guru apparently was most upset that Wilson had changed a handful of his precious words.

Wilson often said that hosting the Family put him out $100,000, including drained credit cards and damage to his cars. He said he spent more than $1,000 (about $7,000 in today's money) for a steady flow of penicillin to treat the free-loving group's rampant venereal diseases. "It was probably the largest gonorrhea bill in history," Wilson said. Despite all that, the drummer arranged an audition for Manson with Terry Melcher, an L.A. record producer (the Byrds, Glen Campbell, the Mamas & the Papas) and son of singer-actress Doris Day. He also arranged studio time for Manson to cut his own demo tracks. Those recordings have never been released so the quality is unknown, but Manson left his mark on those who witnessed the sessions. The sound engineer that day, Stephen Desper, said of the wannabe rock star: "This guy is psychotic."

Manson then stalked away from his relationship with Dennis Wilson, but whatever legacy he had as a musician, he owed it to Wilson's connections. Several rock 'n' roll acts have recorded songs by or about Manson, mostly for shock value, but he does have a musical footprint deep enough that Neil Young, who met Manson through Dennis Wilson, tipped his hat in his 2013 autobiography:

> His songs were off-the-cuff things he made up as he went along, and they were never the same twice in a row. Kind of like Dylan, but different because it was hard to glimpse a true message in them, but the songs were fascinating. He was quite good.

Yet Manson never lost his anger over what he perceived as Wilson's broken promise to get him a record contract through Terry Melcher, which would become a pivotal part of the Family's future.

Inglorious End

As for Dennis Wilson, his life decisions didn't improve after the Manson clan evacuated in its black school bus. He had a moment

Terry Melcher was an L.A. record producer and the son of Doris Day. He was asked to arrange studio time for Manson to cut his own demo tracks, a dangerous assignment.

of glory in 1971, as co-star with James Taylor in the road-buddy film *Two-Lane Blacktop*, but he could never crawl out from under his addictions. The last of his five marriages seemed intended to infuriate his nemesis bandmate, Mike Love. He seduced Love's daughter—his second cousin—when she was 16, then married her when she got pregnant. They were soon estranged.

He lost his seat in the Beach Boys in the early 1980s due to his addictions and erratic behavior, and his life hung in the balance on December 22, 1983, when he checked into a Santa Monica hospital for a 21-day detox/rehab program. A doctor there later said Wilson admitted to drinking a fifth of vodka every day, an eternal buzz that he frosted with cocaine. He left the facility on Christmas Day, then checked into another detox center at 3:30 a.m. on December 26, walking out of that one sometime after the sun came up.

Wilson spent the final night of his life aboard a friend's boat at Marina Del Rey, adjacent to Venice Beach. He was a familiar figure around the marina, where he docked his 62-foot boat, *Harmony*, until he had to sell it to cover his debts. By 9 a.m. on December 28 he was tapping the vodka, and by noon he was "staggering around pretty good," an attendant later told reporters. At 3 p.m., a few people watched Wilson as he began making a series of dives at his old boat slip, clearing debris he found underwater there, then at 4:15 the watchers lost sight of him. They thought he was fooling around—hiding for a laugh—but panic gradually set in, and divers began probing the water. His submerged body was found at 5:30. It was on the shallow marina floor at his old slip. The drowning was accidental, but blood samples showed that he was drunk and had traces of cocaine and Valium in his body. Mike Love created a cruel epitaph when, in the final years of Wilson's life, he labeled his former bandmate "a drugged-out, no-talent parasite."

CHAPTER SIX

Home on
the Range

A scant 30 miles (48 km) from downtown Los Angeles, Topanga Canyon Boulevard rises up out of suburban Chatsworth toward a sparse badlands landscape, where the gnarly fingers of the Santa Susana Mountains reach toward the Pacific. The vistas just west of the boulevard, off an old mountain pass road, will seem familiar to connoisseurs of vintage cowboy movies. A make-believe ranch there—one of several in the immediate vicinity—was used for dozens of studio shoots during the heyday of Hollywood westerns, including *Duel in the Sun*, the 1946 David O. Selznick epic starring Gregory Peck. Wallace Beery, Hoot Gibson, Tom Mix, Roy Rogers, and the Cisco Kid all tromped along the boardwalk of the fake Main Street.

Other scenes were shot amid the boulders, creeks, and caves at the rugged edges of the vast acreage. The venue showed up in episodes of many TV serials as well, including *Bonanza*, *Roy Rogers*, *Zorro*, and *The Lone Ranger*. It was convenient both for the studios and the many actors who lived in the hills. Clayton Moore could holler a final "Hi-yo, Silver," doff his mask, and be home in Calabasas 15 minutes later for cocktail hour.

Two years after Selznick filmed his famous duel there, a Philadelphia native bitten by the movie bug bought the film ranch from William S. Hart, a cowboy star in silent films. Like tens of thousands of other economically stymied Americans, George Spahn had moved west to the Golden State in the 1930s. The Great Depression had upended his comfortable life as a dairy farmer in Lansdale, Pennsylvania, so he pivoted in California from bovine to equine. He built a modest horse empire that included everything from children's pony rides to steed rentals for parades and fairs to providing both stock and wranglers for

The Spahn Movie Ranch, sprawling and dilapidated home to the Manson Family during the late 1960s.

western movies. Spahn Movie Ranch had a good run into the early 1960s, but tastes changed. It was open as a tourist attraction until 1965 when, for a buck, visitors could tour the grounds, watch actors perform horseback stunts and pose for photos with minor stars and make-believe cowboys and Indians. Year by year, as income declined, the old place fell ever deeper into disrepair, finally limping along with hourly horseback-riding trails, with a few hired cowboys tending a herd of 60 animals. Spahn, pushing 80, was on a cane and nearly blind. He lived alone in a decrepit, filthy little house at the head of the property, which had been invaded by rodents and other varmints and seemed at risk of tumbling over at a wolf's huff and puff. Buildings along the old western boardwalk were in no better shape.

Gay Talese wrote this grim description for *Esquire:*

Around the street set, on the edge of the clearing near the trees, are smaller broken-down shacks lived in by wranglers or itinerants who drift to this place periodically and work briefly at some odd job and then disappear. There is an atmosphere of impermanence and neglect about the place, the unwashed windows, the rotting wood, the hauling trucks parked on inclines because their batteries are low and need the momentum of a downhill start.

Hippie Guests

By 1968, Spahn Ranch was facing multiple invasions. Kids from the suburbs were sneaking up to party in the ranch caves and skinny-dip in the creek, and the mountains near L.A. were crawling with hippies, some looking to pitch a tent for a few days, others looking for a more permanent place to build a commune. It didn't take long for them to find Spahn's place. The details of how the Manson Family made its way there are obscure. By some accounts, Lynette Fromme announced in the summer of 1968: "Hey, I found us a ranch!" Others say it was Sandra Good who made the connection much earlier in 1968, even before she joined the Family. Unlike most squatters, Good is said to have approached Spahn and asked whether she and a few friends could camp there. Even with his failing eyesight, Spahn couldn't resist an attractive young woman.

While some members spent time at the ranch that summer, the Family apparently arrived en masse in August or September, after wearing out its welcome at Dennis Wilson's. While Family membership was fluid, it would reach its peak population at the ranch. Spahn's place had many buildings, from shacks to small houses, that could be converted into funky living quarters. Leslie Van Houten described the sleeping arrangements in the old house that the Family claimed:

There were two bedrooms. One was set down further than the rest of the house. It was nothing but one big mattress. We would jump into the room and roll around and do tumbling. This is where most of us slept . . . I say most of us because generally there would be someone who didn't want to sleep with everybody, mainly due to the fact that they were new to the Family. Actually, it's lots of fun to sleep with lots of people and make love in large numbers, too. For these new people, the other bedroom was made into a "shy room."

George Spahn after being told that former tenants of his property were suspects in the Tate–LaBianca murders.

Earning Their Keep

George Spahn had a couple of motivations for allowing the Family to stay. First, they helped out with his horse-riding business. Some customers had complained that his rugged wranglers were sexually harassing female riders who'd come up from Los Angeles, so Manson's women could be better ambassadors. Mostly, though, he enjoyed their company, because he was lonely. He had abandoned a marriage (and, according to biographers, as many as 11 children, each named after a favorite horse) in the 1950s, his romance with his movie ranch business partner, Ruby Pearl, had gone south, and the old man lived alone in a house badly in need of attention.

Some of the tabloid accounts of Manson's time at the ranch suggested that Lynette Fromme and others serviced Spahn sexually, but I doubt his relationship with the women advanced beyond flirting. (Spahn gave Fromme her famous nickname, "Squeaky," because she gave out a little squeal when he affectionately squeezed her leg.) He seemed more grandfatherly than dirty old man, in his cowboy hat, starched white shirt, and uniform work slacks braced by suspenders. Fromme became his favorite Family emissary, and she seemed to love him back. In a poem she wrote in 1971, Fromme described Spahn as "a gentleman, a mountain man, an Irish rogue, and a German businessman." A housekeeper, not so much. One of the women's first chores in his grungy bungalow was to scrape a decade's worth of grease off his old stove.

They fed him several times a day, often beginning with day-old dumpster-dive sweets in the morning. Like Manson, Spahn had a downhome palate. Charlie thought a hunk of Velveeta, a can of fruit cocktail, and a Payday candy bar was eating high on the hog. He was also an obsessive drinker of soda water, which he regarded as a great luxury. His women reckoned his tastes were informed by the deprivation he suffered both as a child and in prison, where a Payday was a kingly treat. Spahn was happy to dine on cheap hot dogs (which the women cut into bite-sized pieces for him, as a mother would for a child) and almost anything found in a grocery store can—stew, chili, beans.

Ultimate Hippie Idyll

For half a year, the Manson Family and Spahn had a mutually beneficial arrangement. Spahn was doted on by attractive young women, like daily visits from the sweet bird of youth, and the Family lived rent-free on a 500-acre ranch that was the ultimate hippie nature idyll, even though it was barely a 15-minute cross-country walk down the slope to the suburban tract homes of Chatsworth. Today, the sprawl has choked in even closer; a vast apartment complex sits across the road from the old ranch entrance, and traffic buzzes by a quarter-mile to the north on the six-lane Ronald Reagan Freeway. But the natural landscape hasn't changed much in the 50 years since the Family lived there. The same tawny-colored sandstone ridges and outcroppings are cut through with the same deep canyons. And the range is dabbed with color—verdant leaves, purple thistle, the mauve of coastal sagebrush, the white flowers of greasewood, wild buckwheat and laurel sumac, the golden *amarillo* of wild mustard weed. Spring rains broaden the palette with the oranges of tiger lilies and monkey flowers, and along the moist draws and creeks dense elderberry bushes tussle for air space with a brigade of looming trees—black walnuts, willows, live oaks, sycamores.

Old film footage shows a flouncy battalion of Manson hippie chicks strolling past sandstone outcroppings and boulders, singing a multi-harmonic version of one of their idol's tunes, "Home Is Where You're Happy." ("So burn all your bridges/Leave your old life far behind you/Just as long as you've got love in your heart/You'll never be alone.") Other shots show them bathing communally in a creek pool. Roughly a year before Manson's group took its grotesque violent turn, they seemed happy and content. After spending more than a year living out of the VW van or the school bus, flopping at one place or another from a few days to a few months, Spahn's place let them expand and breathe. Manson outlawed calendars and clocks, declaring, "There is nothing to do but make love"— which they often did, as a group, after dinner in the movie set's old saloon, bare except for a few dirty mattresses tossed onto the plywood floor.

Fromme wrote of the sensory experience she had at Spahn's:

The ranch gave us texture. The sharp rocks and smooth stones, the sticks and grasses beneath our bare feet, the hoot of an owl, even the distant scent of a skunk all add dimension to our experience. The sun heated the mountain boulders above us by mid-morning, and rattlesnakes lay between them. In the deep, cooler places along the creek, beneath thick-trunked oaks, were shade and dark, moist dirt that felt and smelled good, but also insects, spiders, and poison oak to keep us aware. The medicinal scent of eucalyptus trees cut through the summer humidity, and their rattling signaled a welcome breeze to otherwise sweltering afternoons.

Gregg Jakobson, an L.A. songwriter who got to know the Family through Dennis Wilson, had his own lyrical description of the ranch: "the girls and the guys and the horses and the trucks and the brown grass and the blue sky and the stream." David Dalton, who spent time there, called it "an almost biblical landscape, a perfect setting for Charlie's apocalyptic plans."

The women spent their days sewing clothes—including an elaborate "ceremonial vest" for Manson—and caring for the Family's children, beginning with the arrival in April 1968 of Valentine, known as Pooh Bear, Mary Brunner's child with Manson. (A second boy, named Zezozose, was born at Spahn Ranch six months later, on October 7, to Susan Atkins. She said the baby was delivered by Manson "along with fifteen other girls.")

How did the Family manage to feed 35 people, including children? The numbers add up quickly: 100 meals a day, 700 a week, 3,000 a month. In his memoir, Paul Watkins described the finances:

> *Economically, we managed well. Much of our food came from garbage runs in the valley, or from money derived panhandling. Mary [Brunner] had a contact at a local bakery in Santa Monica who supplied us with bread, cakes, cookies, and other assorted pastries. Several of the girls had credit cards we used for gasoline. Charlie's scams in the city always netted us old cars and donations. People were always giving Charlie things, people like Dennis Wilson and Bobby Beausoleil, who contributed not only*

money, but automobiles, clothing, and food. Meanwhile, all bank accounts became communal property, so that we generally had a reserve of cash when we needed it.

Garbage Runs

The garbage runs are part of Manson Family lore. Fromme explained that the genesis of dumpster diving came from a conversation she had with an older hippie named Zeb at the Spiral Staircase, the Topanga Canyon flophouse. It happened during a loaves-and-fishes moment on the morning after a big party. Everyone woke up hungry, and Fromme was feeling pressure to feed them. Suddenly, she said, old dude Zeb "dropped word that you could get good eats out of supermarket garbage bins." A group set out and confirmed his wisdom. That random tip, Fromme wrote, "was to feed us for years." They favored high-end grocers in high-end cities, like Malibu. Fromme described the process:

> *We girls crept behind Malibu's markets, poking pinched fingers into the bins, and barely touching the piles of surplus food. Then we spied things worth a climb inside: crates of fresh fruits of which some, but not all, had bruises or spots, boxes of lettuce, onions, avocadoes, tomatoes, and peppers. It was good, nutritious food, and there was only one reason much of it had been tossed away: people didn't want to buy a small stalk of celery or a tomato with a bruise. They wanted picture-perfect goods and left the crooked carrots to us . . . We were continually surprised by what we found: sealed blocks of cheese with a few tiny specks of mold; dented or*

misprinted packages of such things as crackers and pasta; dozens of cartons of cold, fresh eggs on ice, all but one or two intact, albeit a little sticky. We brought it all home, separated it, washed it thoroughly, and set about at different tables to pare it down for pizzas, spaghetti, and stews that fed dozens. We had real butter, bread, and bright, crisp salads, and we came to believe that you could have fed the world with just America's garbage.

I must add that in another reminiscence of life on the ranch, Fromme admitted that the truth was less wholesome: "While maintaining a façade of normalcy, some of the girls became bulimic and anorexic . . . and a lot of people were overeating donuts."

Early Acolytes

Manson's group expanded and contracted from week to week as some came, some left, and still others returned. This included the original core of five or six, including Brunner, Fromme and a few others who spent time with Manson in northern California or in early journeys in his Volkswagen van, before they supersized to the bus.

With a few exceptions, most members were southern Californians from the Los Angeles region. Who were they? Though it has become a cliché, many of the young women had, in fact, grown up in "broken homes," bearing the psychological damage that can accompany divorce. Most were born just after World War II, when divorce was still relatively uncommon. (The overall divorce rate in the U.S. was about 25 percent in 1950; it would climb to 50 percent by the mid-1970s.)

In addition to Brunner and Fromme, Manson's early acolytes included Susan Atkins, the comely brunette who was mesmerized by Manson after he showed up with a guitar at her communal house in San Francisco. Ella Jo Bailey, another of Manson's earliest followers, apparently knew Atkins from the San Francisco hippie scene and impulsively joined her friend when she set off with the guitar-slinging ex-con.

Patricia Krenwinkel, the fifth core follower, had a similarly troubled biography. She was born in 1947 in Inglewood, another Los Angeles suburb, where her father sold insurance. Her parents would later describe their daughter as "exceedingly normal," to the extent that her childhood included Campfire Girls and Bible School—as American as apple pie. But the family's veneer began to peel after her parents split in 1964, when Patricia was 17. Her mother returned to her native Alabama, but Patricia stayed in L.A. to finish high school, living with her father and older half-sister, Charlene.

Patricia says she had a miserable adolescence as she was depressed and self-conscious about being overweight and homely. She says she was prescribed amphetamines and that Charlene introduced her to marijuana and alcohol. After high school she took a cheap apartment with her sister in El Porto, near the beach, where she learned that her sister was a heroin addict. She was also pregnant, and Patricia says she cared for her newborn nephew for several months. Like Atkins, Krenwinkel met Manson while he was playing a guitar. He happened to be at the home of a friend of her sister. Krenwinkel invited him home, and they slept together that night. She said Manson expressed his love, and she says she wept over the idea that anyone would feel affectionate toward her. Two days later, she quit her job, abandoned her sister and her nephew, and joined Brunner, Fromme, Atkins, and Bailey as lovers and devotees of the little ex-convict.

Manson's Other Women

About a dozen other men and women formed the nucleus of the Family during its stay at Spahn Ranch. Primary among them was Leslie Van Houten, another child of Los Angeles, who was born there in 1949 to a schoolteacher mother and a car-salesman father. She was an all-American girl—a high school athlete and homecoming princess who followed a prudent, practical path to secretarial school—but the counterculture beckoned, and she slipped out of the mainstream and into recreational drug usage. While in Berkeley in the summer of 1968, Van Houten became acquainted with a young couple from Los Angeles, Bobby and Gail Beausoleil. Bobby had hung out with the Manson Family, and he invited Van Houten to visit the ranch commune. From that day forward she was never far from Manson's side, and she would become one of his most stubborn defenders.

She had that in common with the self-assured Sandra Good. Although Good joined the Family nearly a year after its conception, no member was more devoted to Manson. Like Brunner, Good had attended college and was among the older female followers, although still a full decade younger than Manson. She was born in 1944 in San Diego, the youngest of three girls, and her father, a stockbroker, split with her mother when she was four years old. Like so many, she joined the Family on the invitation of other members. She began following Manson in April 1968 and truly never stopped—

even long after the murders and criminal prosecutions had prompted all but Lynette Fromme to abandon the cause. Lithe, finely featured, fair-skinned and auburn-haired, Good might have been mistaken for Fromme's older sister. The two would become fast, longtime friends.

Ruth Ann Moorehouse, born in 1951, was one of Manson's youngest followers. They had an unusual mode of meeting: Her father, who was religious, picked up the hitchhiking Manson, Brunner, and Fromme and brought them home for dinner. As his 16-year-old daughter made goo-goo eyes at Manson, father Dean Moorehouse gave him a piano, which he traded for a Volkswagen van. Ruth Ann then joined the Family for a trip north to Mendocino. Her father fetched her home and threatened to kill Manson, but there was no keeping her away.

Another core member, Catherine Share, had swarthy skin, black hair, and dark eyes that gave her an exotic look—and the nickname Gypsy. Share traveled a long and interesting journey to find Manson. She is said to have been born in Paris in 1942, during World War II, to a Hungarian violinist father and a German mother, who were members of the French Resistance. Biographers have said that her parents committed suicide in 1944, shortly before the Allied liberation of Western Europe. The girl was adopted by a French woman who emigrated to California and married an American psychologist. Biographers have reported that her adoptive mother committed suicide after a cancer diagnosis when Catherine was 16. Another friend of Bobby Beausoleil, she joined the counterculture in San Francisco after finishing Hollywood High School, and she too joined the Family at Spahn Ranch.

Linda Drouin Kasabian, born in 1949 in coastal Maine, was another rare Mansonite who was not born in southern California. A high school dropout whose parents had divorced when she was young, Kasabian was twice-married by the time she joined Manson's ranch commune in the fall of 1968. She arrived with a 16-month-old daughter, Tanya, after meeting Catherine Share at a Topanga Canyon hippie house. Kasabian came to the Family late, but she became a pivotal member as wheelwoman for the Tate and LaBianca kill teams. She was among the first to turn against Manson, earning the vitriol of the diminutive guru and his still-ardent followers.

Kasabian was welcomed to the Family by ritual sex with Manson in a Spahn Ranch cave. She said it featured Charlie's usual rap about her "father hang-up," which she recounted in a courtroom exchange with an attorney:

Q: What conversation did you have with Mr. Manson while you were making love?

Kasabian: I don't recall the entire conversation, but he told me I had a father hang-up.

Q: Did this impress you when he said you had a father hang-up?

Kasabian: Very much so.

Q: Why?

Kasabian: Because nobody ever said that to me, and I did have a father hang-up. I hated my stepfather.

Kasabian said Manson "could see right through me." His women apparently did not share their notes about Manson's pillow talk, though. If they had, they would have known that he used make-love-to-daddy with each of them.

Family Guys

While Manson was the undisputed leading man of the Family, a handful of other young males—known to the women as "our guys"—had supporting roles. One was handsome Bobby Beausoleil, a heart-throb of many of the women. Beausoleil was born in 1947 in Santa Barbara, a coastal city that sits in the lap of the Santa Ynez Mountains, two hours from Los Angeles. A talented musician and an aspiring actor and artist, he rebelled in high school and, after a reform school stint, split from his milkman father. He performed in bands in L.A. and San Francisco and stumbled into the Family one night during a party at the Spiral Staircase. (Beausoleil was married but had an open relationship with his wife, Gail, who became a familiar figure at the ranch.)

In her autobiography, Fromme admitted that Beausoleil tickled her in all the right places. She described his grand entrance at the party: "Neither small nor baby-faced—but fine, according to us girls—in a top hat and cape, bobbing through the doorway blowing an instrument he called a kaliedesoon in trickling notes that ran up and down the spines of the dancers, faster and faster until I blanked out."

It seems Beausoleil had his own way of inspiring frisson. Years later, in an interview, he testily staked his own flag as a major sexual player in the Family. "It didn't seem like a guy with his harem," Beausoleil insisted. "There were always other guys there. Although I would say that Manson was the figurehead of whatever group existed at any given time, characterizing them

Under pressure: Bobby Beausoleil talks to newsmen after the jury returned a verdict of first-degree murder in the torture slaying of musician Gary Hinman.

as his harem isn't at all accurate." Beausoleil was one of the few
Manson followers who was earning a legitimate living, which he
did between his music and an occasional film role, including a
soft-core porn film (subtly entitled *The Ramrodder*), shot in part
at the Spahn Ranch and also featuring Catherine Share.

Another of "our guys" was Paul Watkins, the Family's little
brother, who had perpetually glazed-over eyes and marijuana
giggles. His father was in the oil business, and he led a nomadic
childhood in the Middle East and on the Texas Gulf Coast before
his family settled into the L.A. exurb of Thousand Oaks. He then
discovered the counterculture and dropped out of high school as
a 17-year-old senior, abandoning his position as class president
and his status as an evangelical Christian. A few months later, in
March 1968, he bumped into the Family while tent-camping in
Topanga Canyon, at the time they were flopping at the Spiral
Staircase. Watkins, another good musician, was a prototype
speaker of the SoCal stoner-surfer patois that Sean Penn's Jeff
Spicoli character vocalized in *Fast Times at Ridgemont High*: "Hey,
bud, let's party!" Watkins crossed paths with the Family a second
time during an orgy at Dennis Wilson's house, and he became a
bona fide member at the Spahn Ranch, where he had his oral sex
tête-à-tête with Manson.

The youngest of the men was Steve Grogan, who joined
the commune at Spahn on about his 17th birthday. He apparently
grew up in the Los Angeles area and dropped out of high school
early. The Family found him looming at the edges of the ranch,
ogling the bare-chested women on their daily constitutionals,
then scooting around a boulder and disappearing when they
approached. Manson finally wrangled him into the herd. He

wasn't particularly handsome, with a mouthful of jagged, broken teeth, a chinstrap of juvenile whiskers, and hair the color of dirty straw, but he was a tall, strapping teenager, broad at the shoulders and narrow at the hips. The Family's women learned that Grogan had a teen's libido—and a permanent boner.

Fromme wrote:

Some of us were shy of him because he had no pretense. He wanted to make love to all of us—not just to lie down, but to steal the moments when we stood on the boardwalk stalking, to slide up, wrap his arms around us, and move us like Charlie did . . . Steven came into our circle . . . He came into our bed. It was a marriage of sorts. He was smart, tender, and funny.

Fromme said the women encouraged Grogan to put on a hillbilly accent, and that led to two nicknames: Clem and Scramblehead. Whether Grogan was smart, as Fromme contends, or an ignoramus, as others say, is an open question. In any case, he played the fool well. A judge would later treat him leniently, declaring: "It's clear Grogan functions barely above the animal level."

Another of "our guys," Charles Watson, followed his own serpentine journey into the Family. He was among the older followers, arriving in his mid-20s. Watson was born in 1945, the youngest of three children of churchy parents from small-town Texas, 50 miles (80 km) north of Dallas. (Naturally, he was nicknamed Tex by Manson.) After a no-drama childhood as a sports star with honor-roll grades, Watson began to drift from the straight and narrow in college. He then dropped out and after a few detours landed in California, where he and a friend tried to make a living selling wigs at a short-lived Malibu store they called Love Locs.

Lynette Fromme said of Watson: "He was so personable he could have sold homes, cars, magazines, or anything but wigs on southern California beaches. He was politely aggressive, interested in girls, and ultra-confident, even with the aw-shucks guffaw."

Watson turned to marketing a new product, marijuana, and met the Family at Dennis Wilson's house, reportedly after picking up the hitchhiking Beach Boy. He lived at the ranch commune in the fall of 1968, withdrew into the real world that winter, then returned to the Family in March 1969. Rejoining was a momentous decision. By the date of his return, Manson's priorities had shifted from peace and love to doomsday prepping.

Back on the Road

At the same time, the welcome wagon at the ranch had pulled away from the Manson Family, which returned to its natural state of itinerancy. One impetus was a growing conflict with a ranch cowboy, a Massachusetts native named Donald Shea who had moved to L.A. after a stint in the Air Force in the 1950s, aiming to work in western movies. He drove a truck emblazoned with his name and occupation: "FAMOUS MOVIE AND TV STUNTMAN." (Fromme shivved him in her book, quipping he was "stellar in his own mind.") His specialties were straight out of the western scriptwriter's narrative playbook: the gallows drop and death falls, neck drags and foot drags from moving horses. But his film employment, always meager, dwindled further with the declining popularity of western shoot-'em-ups. Shea was an

Charles (Tex) Watson—according to Fromme, "He was so personable he could have sold homes, cars, magazines or anything but wigs on southern California beaches."

imposing man—beefy and more than a foot taller than Manson at 6 ft 4 in (1.93 m), which gave him the ironic nickname of Shorty. He didn't trust the Family in general and Manson in particular, seeing him as a lazy, freeloading, con man. And he shared his opinion freely with George Spahn.

Perhaps not coincidentally, Spahn grew ornery with the Manson women, complaining that trail-riding customers were being scared away by the hippie "bums" wandering the ranch. Late in 1968, he told them to hitch up their bus and get along.

CHAPTER SEVEN

Helter Skelter

In February 1968, the four Beatles trekked to India for a ten-week workshop with the progenitor of mantra-chanting Transcendental Meditation, Maharishi Mahesh Yogi. His ashram was in Rishikesh, a small city on the sacred Ganges, 250 miles (400 km) north of New Delhi in the Himalayan foothills. The band had spent time with the Maharishi in the U.K. at the urging of George Harrison, who had grown captivated by eastern mysticism. They traveled to Rishikesh with an entourage that included wives, girlfriends, and a few other celebrities: Mike Love, the Beach Boys front man; actress Mia Farrow and her sister Prudence; and Donovan Leitch, the Scottish psychedelic pop star ("Sunshine Superman," "Mellow Yellow," "Hurdy Gurdy Man," etc.). The group traded their swinging Sixties threads for kurtas and kurtis, salwar bottoms, and garlands of marigolds.

The complicated interrelationships between the four bandmates—all filthy rich before their 30th birthdays—were growing increasingly fractured, so they collectively decided that a stretch at the ashram might restore their kindredship. As Harrison put it, they were "looking to re-establish that which was within."

But even the Maharishi could not mend the Beatles.

Ringo left after ten days, unable to stomach the ashram food. Paul, who went on a songwriting tear the moment he arrived, also left prematurely—in a snit after Harrison scolded him that they were in Rishikesh to meditate, not make records. John lasted two months but left in disgust amid a toxic rumor that the Maharishi was hitting on the Farrow sisters and other young women.

Team photo with the Maharishi in 1968: (from the left) Patti Boyd, John Lennon, Mike Love (nemesis of Dennis Wilson), Maharishi Mahesh Yogi, George Harrison, Mia Farrow, John Farrow, Donovan, Paul McCartney, Jane Asher, Cynthia Lennon.

White Album Hits the Charts

The band's retreat to India did not result in self-actualization, but the time-out churned up a musical wellspring—a creative burst of five dozen songs, including compositions from all four. They regathered in May at Harrison's home, outside London in Esher, and began sorting through songs for a new LP that would become *The Beatles*, also known as the White Album. They cut 30 tracks over the ensuing four months, which would go into the double-LP. The songs were a disjointed hodgepodge—or, more charitably, creatively diverse. They ranged from strange throwaway fragments like "Wild Honey Pie" to the self-indulgent eight minutes of random noise entitled "Revolution 9." The record also included such radio hits as "Back in the U.S.S.R.," "Ob-La-Di, Ob-La-Da," "Birthday," and Harrison's masterful musical meditation on the band's (and the world's) disharmony, "While My Guitar Gently Weeps."

Obsessive Listener

The album dropped in the U.K. on November 22, 1968, and a few days later in the U.S. One particular fan in California eagerly awaited its arrival. The Beatles had arrived during Charles Manson's seven-year federal prison stretch, which began in 1960, and the band became his musical inspiration—and object of deranged jealousy. Fellow inmates claim that Manson declared: "Given the chance, I could be bigger than the Beatles."

A few days after the White Album's release, Manson huddled in front of a stereo at a hippie friend's place in Topanga Canyon and drank in all 93 minutes, lost in his own version of musical frisson. After acquiring his own copy he listened obsessively over the next four weeks, committing the lyrics to memory. He drilled down deeply into a handful of songs, including Harrison's angry "Piggies" and three by McCartney: the sweet ballad "Blackbird," the quirky, clever lyrics of "Rocky Raccoon," and his metal-edged rocker, "Helter Skelter." Manson then took a giant step over the line of sanity as he grew convinced that the Beatles were directly communicating with him through the record.

Even 50 years along, the idea that Manson was having a transcendent musical conversation with Paul McCartney will often summon sniggers. It might seem prima facie bananas, but isn't transcendence a function of music? As Yip Harburg, a brilliant American pop lyricist from the 1930s, put it: "Words make you think a thought. Music makes you feel a feeling. A song makes you feel a thought." (His song catalog offers tangible proof: "Somewhere Over the Rainbow," "April in Paris," "Brother, Can You Spare a Dime?" et al.)

Hidden Messages

As early as 1966, the Beatles had begun toying with backmasking, the recording technique of leaving messages that are revealed when a record or tape is played in reverse. The fadeout at the end of "Rain," the trippy B-side of "Paperback Writer," is tagged with a few seconds of John Lennon singing backwards. And a year after the White Album, the alleged "Paul is dead" backmasking on *Abbey Road* caused an international sensation. College students everywhere earnestly studied earlier Beatles records for similar messaging, and some claimed to hear "Turn me on, dead man" in the noise of "Revolution 9."

Even beyond this whimsy, haven't music enthusiasts always turned recordings of their favorite artists inside out to find references to something deeper? There were the brassy sexual double-entendres of early "race" music, Billy Strayhorn's sad hints of closeted gayness in "Lush Life," and, on the flip-side of that emotion, Diana Ross's celebratory "I'm Coming Out." What cognizant teenager with a few bucks to spare didn't wear out the grooves on a record while seeking the hidden meanings concealed in the White Album or other iconic deep-consciousness LPs of that era—Jefferson Airplane's *Surrealistic Pillow*, Cream's *Disraeli Gears*, James Taylor's *Sweet Baby James*, Carole King's *Tapestry*, and more? Hell, Bob Dylan's *Subterranean Homesick Blues*, a single that was over in 141 seconds, kept some of us occupied for months.

White Album Blows Manson's Mind

Of course, Manson went far beyond rational analysis. In his fever dream, the Beatles were direct-messaging to him a warning that a race riot was on the horizon, and the Family's survival was at stake. About four weeks after he first heard "Helter Skelter," he began the process of reprogramming his followers away from the love-is-all zeitgeist and toward violence. He preached this new gospel during a memorable gathering on New Year's Eve 1968, far from Los Angeles. From that point forward, according to Leslie Van Houten, "All we did was listen to the Beatles' White Album and read Revelations," the apocalyptic final book of the Bible's New Testament. Manson conflated the Beatles' "Revolution 9" and the Bible's Revelation 9, which warns of hordes of locusts and scorpions (a symbol of world destruction) and hints at refuge in a bottomless pit—a "shaft of the Abyss"—from which a new king would emerge. You guessed it: Manson supposed he would be that king.

As Family relations with George Spahn collapsed in the fall of 1968, a newly arrived member of the commune, 28-year-old Catherine Gillies, suggested a faraway spot in Death Valley as their next home. Her grandparents, Bill and Barbara Myers, had built a small ranch in 1932 on a dead-end road that paralleled Goler Wash, just inside the vast Death Valley National Park, 225 miles (360 km) northeast of Los Angeles and 80 miles (130 km) from the Nevada state line. The Family arrived there in November and soon took over a nearby property that was bigger and in better condition. That ranch was owned by an Oklahoma couple, James and Arlene Barker. The Myers had operated a small gas station and café before retreating back to civilization in Fresno, and the Barkers were involved in mining in the area. (As the crow flies, the ranches are 20 miles (32 km) from Searles Lake, a regional natural wonder. The dry lakebed, crusted in white, has yielded mountains of minerals, including borax and salt.) Manson biographers say he bribed Arlene Barker: She allowed them to squat after he gave her a Beach Boys gold record, a gift to him from Dennis Wilson.

A half-dozen Manson Family memoirists have recounted the cult leader's New Year's Eve sermon in the desert. They all agree "Helter Skelter" was the beginning of Manson's grooming of his followers for murder. He told them, "I would die for you," and then asked: "Would you die for me? Would you kill for me?"

The exception is Lynette Fromme, whose 2018 auto-biography is largely dedicated to minimizing Manson's culpability and dismissing prosecutor/author Vincent Bugliosi's narrative linking the Family murders to "Helter Skelter." Here is her haughty repudiation of the Beatles connection:

> *After we heard the new Beatles album, someone got a Bible to check out passages that struck a chord (and accord). The new Beatles White Album was as appealing as their others, but also different, with specific sounds in their songs, and the same sounds gathered in the piece called "Revolution 9." Most interesting were the sounds of gunfire, the grunts of pigs, the screams and moans of people dying, of people making love, a baby's babble, a black man yelling "Rise!" The album was timely. We believed that the song "Blackbird" was written for the black race. We chuckled on* hearing "Sexy Sadie" [which they linked to Susan Atkins' nickname, Sadie], *and wept with George Harrison's guitar.* [It was Eric Clapton's guitar, actually.] *We acknowledged the genius that had created the album, but we did not believe that the Beatles were talking to us, unless you included us in the soul of the world. The album was just interesting.*

Fromme has spent 50 years entombed in a bubble of her own reality, but she stands apart from other former Family members, who agree that the White Album blew Manson's mind. He believed the Beatles were counting on the Family to produce a response record.

"Death Valley marked a turning point for the Manson Family," Paul Watkins wrote. "It is not easy to make sense of what happened there. I can only describe my own experience of it. But I do believe that coming to the desert stamped the fate of

the family, and subsequently, the fate of its victims." He quoted
Manson's New Year's Eve sermon, delivered as the Family
gathered around a roaring campfire on that frigid desert night:

> *Are you hip to what the Beatles are saying? . . . Dig it, they're
> telling it like it is. They know what's happening in the city;
> blackie is getting ready. They put the revolution to music . . .
> "Helter Skelter" is coming down. Hey, their album is getting the
> young love [America's youth] ready, man, building up steam.
> Our album is going to pop the cork right out of the bottle.*

Search for Nirvana

Charles (Tex) Watson analyzed Manson's rap in his own memoir:

> *Los Angeles and all the other pig cities would be in flames.
> It would be the apocalypse, the deserved judgment on the whole
> sick establishment that hated us and all the other free children,
> the establishment that had cheated Charlie out of his genius.
> While the rich piggies lay butchered on their own manicured
> front lawns, we would have found safety. Charlie would have
> led us through a secret Devil's Hole into the Bottomless Pit:
> an underground paradise beneath Death Valley where water
> from a lake would give everlasting life and you could eat fruit
> from twelve magical trees—a different one for each month of
> the year.*

Watson said the hyperactive Manson grew ever more mercurial
in the desert, leading frantic searches in stolen dune buggies

for the magical underground entrance to their fountain of youth. They spent days traversing the desert looking for this Nirvana, where Manson believed his following would grow to the biblically mandated 144,000-strong. These details would become important points of the district attorney's narrative of Manson's delusions.

Again, Fromme served as a retrospective Manson translator, sanding the edges of his craziness.

> *Prosecutors would inflate the ideas, claiming that our plan was to emerge like cicadas years later without having physically aged. In their story, Charlie intended to rise as king, Jesus, God. Hogwash. Charlie was looking at underground tunnels and caves to hide from the insane people who would destroy their own planet in pursuit of gold and oil. He inspired me in a sense of adventure that supplanted paralyzing dread. If chaos was inevitable, we would ride it out on top of our fears rather than cringing beneath them. We would do what was needed to survive.*

Jailhouse Interview

But Manson expounded on the very details that Fromme dismissed—willfully ignorant of the man she spent her lifetime idolizing. He would give hundreds of interviews over his lifetime, and many were marked—and marred—by his bewildering obfuscations and put-ons. But a jailhouse interview in 1970 with Dalton of *Rolling Stone* was more unguarded and unrehearsed—an approximation of honesty, in other words. A few excerpts of their exchange:

Dalton: Can you explain the meaning of Revelations, Chapter 9?
Manson: What do you think it means? It's the battle of Armageddon. It's the end of the world. It was the Beatles' "Revolution 9" that turned me on to it. It predicts the overthrow of the Establishment. The pit will be opened, and that's when it will all come down. A third of all mankind will die. The only people who escape will be those who have the seal of God on their foreheads. You know that part, "They will seek death but they will not find it."

Dalton: How do you know that these things are coming about?
Manson: I'm just telling you what my awareness sees. I look into the future like an Indian on a trail. I know what my senses tell me. I can just see it coming, and when it comes, I will just say, "Hi there!"

Dalton: Why do you think that this revolution predicted in "Revolution 9" will be violent? Why will it be racial?
Manson: Have you heard of the Muslims? Have you heard of the Black Panthers? . . . You and all Western man killed and mutilated them and now they are reincarnated, and they are going to repay you. The soul in the white man is lying down.

Dalton: Can you explain the prophecies you found in the Beatles' double album?
Manson: At the end of each song there is a little tag piece on it, a couple of notes. Or like in "Piggies" there's "oink, oink, oink." Just these couple of sounds. And all these sounds are repeated in

"Revolution 9." Like in "Revolution 9," all these pieces are fitted together and they predict the violent overthrow of the white man. Like you'll hear "oink, oink," and then right after that, machine gun fire. AK-AK-AK-AK-AK-AK! . . . "Revolution 9" referred to Revelations Chapter 9. It's the battle of Armageddon. It's the end of the world.

Dalton: Do you really think the Beatles intended to mean that?
Manson: I think it's a subconscious thing. I don't know whether they did or not. But it's there. It's an association in the subconscious. This music is bringing on the revolution, the unorganized overthrow of the Establishment. The Beatles know in the sense that the subconscious knows.

Dalton: What does "Rocky Raccoon" mean?
Manson: Coon. You know, that's a word they use for black people. You know the line, "Gideon checked out and he left it no doubt/ to help with good Rocky's revival." Rocky's revival—re-vival. It means coming back to life. The black man is going to come back into power again. "Gideon checks out" means that it's all written out there in the New Testament, in the Book of Revelations . . .

And so forth, ad nauseam. But sitting around a fire on that cold New Year's Eve night, Manson's followers nodded in agreement as he spun this story, knitting White Album lyric fragments and random words into a quixotic narrative. As ex-Family member Dianne Lake said: "Charlie had this ability to make sense out of nonsense."

Claims Credit for White Album Songs

He claimed the song "I Will" referenced a Manson recording in its lyric: "Your song will fill the air/Sing it loud so I can hear you." He said "Honey Pie," which mentioned "the magic of your Hollywood song," was a message beckoning him to London: "You are driving me frantic/Sail across the Atlantic/To be where you belong." Manson took credit for many of the White Album song concepts and even specific lyrics. One example was John Lennon's "Sexy Sadie." Manson had given the nickname Sadie Mae Glutz to Susan Atkins years before the record dropped, so he claimed credit for it.

Nor does the magical messaging hold up for the other songs. Harrison wrote "Piggies" as a protest against corporate greed, and McCartney's "Blackbird" was a homage to the American civil rights movement (or to a bird outside his room at the ashram; McCartney gave different explanations). In "Rocky Raccoon," McCartney was showing off his clever lyrical chops in a song inspired by the nickname of Kwasi (Rocky) Dzidzornu, a Ghanaian-born English percussionist who performed with many major American and English rock stars.

And then there was "Helter Skelter." In a 2018 TV interview, McCartney explained that its genesis had everything to do with rock and roll machismo and nothing to do with war and revolution. He said that he read a music-industry newspaper story in 1968 reporting that The Who had gone into the studio and cut a "dirty, filthy, loud" single. (McCartney said he was never able to discern the title of the song, so it may have gone unreleased.) In any case, McCartney said, he told his bandmates:

"We've got to make a song that's dirtier and filthier and louder than The Who." And "Helter Skelter" was born.

Race Riots

Manson may have rounded the bend of sanity with his Beatles imaginings, but he was cunning in hitching his otherwise mad design for murder to a looming "race war." After five years of riots in American cities (and the attendant white flight to the suburbs), the activist Stokely Carmichael's concept of "black power" was roiling society by 1969. Civil rights protests began in May 1963 in Birmingham, Alabama, when the city's large black underclass took to the streets to fight back against a series of bombings by the Ku Klux Klan, who were protected by the all-white local police force. The Klan's intention was to induce terror in minorities.

The summer of 1964 brought race riots to New York City and several New Jersey suburbs, as well as to Chicago, Philadelphia, and Rochester, New York, and a new baseline was created by the devastating violence in the Watts section of Los Angeles in August 1965. Touched off by a simple white-on-black police arrest, week-long rioting left 34 dead, 1,000 injured, and 4,000 arrested.

"Long, hot summer" rioting in big cities was institutionalized by 1967, with widespread violence in June, July, and August from one corner of the country to the other—there were riots in Atlanta, Boston, Cincinnati, Houston, and New York, as well as Newark, New Jersey; Buffalo, New York; Tampa, Florida; Detroit and several other Michigan cities; Tucson, Arizona; Milwaukee, Wisconsin; Minneapolis, Minnesota; and Portland, Oregon.

In the spring of 1968, while the Manson Family was lolling naked around Dennis Wilson's mansion, city streets in Washington, D.C., New York, Chicago, Detroit, Pittsburgh, Pennsylvania, Louisville, Kentucky, and elsewhere were ablaze amid outrage over the April 4 assassination of Martin Luther King Jr. in Memphis.

The Black Panthers

The United States government launched investigations to place blame for the rioting, and J. Edgar Hoover, the FBI's boss-for-life, was unequivocal. He stood before the press and declared: "The Black Panther party, without question, represents the greatest threat to the internal security of the country."

He continued:

> *Schooled in the Marxist-Leninist ideology and the teachings of Chinese Communist leader Mao Zedong, its members have perpetrated numerous assaults on police officers and have engaged in violent confrontations with police in cities throughout the country. Leaders and representatives of the Black Panther party travel extensively all over the United States preaching their gospel of hate and violence not only to ghetto residents, but to students in colleges, universities, and high schools, as well.*

The Panthers were founded in 1966 by Bobby Seale and Huey Newton as a citizens' brigade to monitor the Oakland, California, police department, which had been accused of brutalizing African Americans. At its peak, the group had perhaps 3,000 active members scattered among a half-dozen big-city branches and 50 smaller outposts. By some lights, the Panthers had benevolent goals, including a Robin Hood reputation of feeding the poor. By others, it was populated by too many hotheads, who were quick to draw on both police officers and perceived black rivals.

Behind a curtain of counterintelligence, Hoover did what he could to stir up those rivalries and demonize the organization, ordering his agency to "disrupt, misdirect, discredit, or otherwise neutralize" the Panthers and other "black nationalist hate-type organizations." This message became a drumbeat of war on the front pages of American newspapers. In 1969, the National Urban League led a jet caravan of 15 journalists on a tour of seven cities—all with active Black Panthers chapters—"to give them a view of urban problems from the black neighborhoods rather than from downtown."

John Herbers, a national civil rights correspondent for *The New York Times*, wrote a long account of the unusual tour, during which group interviews were staged with local citizens, as though the reporters were ogling a remote civilization. After one such session in Detroit, Herbers wrote: "The overriding feeling expressed at the meeting was that the police could not be looked to for protection and that the black community, dependent on its own resources, was determined to fight for its interests even if it meant being 'wiped out.'" He added later in the story: "The ultra-militants are biding their time and preparing for the overthrow of the American system, in whatever form that might take."

Well, that was dramatic.

Carl T. Rowan, America's most prominent black newspaper columnist of the era, was a keen observer of this overwrought rhetoric—by Hoover, by national politicians, by black leaders, and by journalists who should have known better. He summarized the dangerous dynamic:

> *The Panthers are hostile, alienated elements of society who have chosen to live by the sword, and millions of Americans will say they deserve to die by the sword. The Panthers are also black. In crying, "Kill the pigs!" and in building up ghetto fortresses filled with machine guns, shotguns and carbines, the Black Panthers have come to symbolize every fear—rational and irrational—that the white American holds for the black American.*

Charles Manson had been perfectly positioned when the hippie chicks descended on San Francisco for the 1967 Summer of Love. Now he was ready to capitalize on the white summer of terror two years later. Since everyone was expecting a race war, Manson told his Family, they would "show blackie how to do it."

CHAPTER EIGHT

Namu Myōhō Renge Kyō

A fter two full years of successfully sponging off his followers and taking advantage of the goodwill of a string of strangers like George Spahn, Charles Manson found himself in a capital crisis as he began prepping for Armageddon, including the happily-ever-after life in (or under) forbidding Death Valley. High temperatures there average above 100°F (38°C) from May through September, and lows frequently dip to freezing in December, January, and February. The Family would need to stockpile deep stores of food and other fundamental provisions, such as fuel and water. But they had limited out the few credit cards that members owned, and there were no high-end grocery dumpsters to dive in Death Valley. The real world was intruding on their dream of hippie utopia.

For the first nine months of 1969, the Family pinballed between several locations—their distant desert retreat, the Spahn Ranch, where they squatted once again whether the owner liked it or not, and the "Yellow Submarine," a rambling banana-colored house on Gresham Street in Canoga Park, a suburb 5 miles (8 km) south down Topanga Canyon Road from Spahn's place.

As the year wore on, Manson grew obsessed with acquiring dune buggies for the desert, so he turned to a favored crime of his youth; auto theft.

The Family stole a number of Volkswagen Beetles, which they then stripped and converted to dune buggies at Spahn Ranch. They cast a wide net for the cars, from stealing off the street to the brand-new VW Bug that Mary Brunner never returned after a phony test drive at a car dealership.

"We began stealing anything we could get our hands on," said Charles (Tex) Watson. "Money, credit cards, traveler's checks, dune buggy parts. It was all for Helter Skelter, Charlie told us; we had to be ready. We creepy-crawled a couple of houses in Malibu and walked off with clothes and some tape equipment that turned out to have already been stolen from NBC."

But Manson knew he would need much more cash to stock the desert hideout. And as the summer of 1969 arrived, this imperative led to the Family's first acts of violence. Much of the moralizing about the gullibility of Manson's followers has been directed at his women—and most of them richly deserved it. But I find it interesting that relatively little scorn has been fixed on Watson, who was the pivot man of the bloodshed. Quite literally, he had a hand in nearly all of it, as we will see.

The Shooting of Lotsapoppa

When Manson wanted quick money, he would badger followers for the names of friends and family members they could target. He knew Watson was intimately involved with a likely candidate. For most of his time with the Family, Watson would come and go because he had a girlfriend in Hollywood who was not interested in immersing herself in the Manson lifestyle. Her name was Rosina Kroner, known for years among Manson biographers by the pseudonym Luella. She lived in an apartment on Franklin Avenue at the base of Hollywood Heights, adjacent to the Magic Castle club, and made a living peddling weed an ounce or two at a time—in an era when you could buy a full kilo for just $100. Manson first asked Watson to squeeze Kroner for a free-will "donation." When she declined, he ordered Watson to use his girlfriend to set up a drug burn.

They fabricated a scheme that no schoolboy would fall for. Watson told Kroner that the Family was working on a bulk marijuana deal with an organized crime connection. He said they would sell 25 kg (55 lbs) for $2,500, plus a $250 fee for Kroner. Believing the sale was on the level, Kroner enlisted a dealer friend, Bernard Crowe, a black man known as Lotsapoppa. Crowe was not the savviest pusher in L.A. He pulled in a financial backer who was supposed to swap cash for the dope—a simple transaction at an L.A. apartment complex—but Watson somehow convinced the bagman to fall for the amateur scam of handing over the cash before he had the marijuana. (In fact, he hadn't even seen the weed.) Watson then slipped out a back door and delivered the cash to Manson.

When Crowe called Spahn Ranch and threatened to kill Rosina Kroner and annihilate the Family, Manson and follower Thomas Walleman went to meet with him at Kroner's apartment on July 1, 1969. It was another predictably bizarre Manson episode. Walleman was supposed to be the triggerman if Crowe got violent, and he was armed with an antique Buntline Special revolver, a long-barreled, Old West-style .22 that had been floating around the Spahn Ranch. But he chickened out, and Manson grabbed the gun. After a back-and-forth with Crowe and what a witness described as the little guru's "ritualistic dance," he pointed the gun at Crowe's abdomen and pulled the trigger. It clicked but didn't fire. Crowe and his pals laughed when it clicked again after a second trigger pull.

"You're crazy!" Crowe said. "Do you come here with an empty gun?" Just as those words left his larynx, Manson jerked the trigger a third time—to full effect. Crowe fell with a bullet wound to his torso.

Manson fled back to the cocoon of his Family, where he recounted his manly act of what he believed to be murder. The next day, according to Charles Watson: "Charlie couldn't stop talking about how he 'plugged blackie.'" In fact, Crowe survived—and would exact his own revenge by testifying against Manson down the line.

The Floodgates Open

The shooting of Lotsapoppa was a crossing of the Rubicon for the Manson Family, a steep escalation of felonious irrationality. Yet there is no record that a single one of them raised a hand to question the path they were charging down. The next step in this progression occurred four weeks later, and the new target was a particularly malicious choice since he was a friend and benefactor of the Family.

I have been writing for more than 40 years about the horrible acts that human beings are capable of committing. My professional body of work includes examinations of perhaps 1,000 murder cases that create a narrative history of the worst of humanity over the past century. A few stand out in my memory. There was the Memphis man who dedicated a karaoke ballad—Willie Nelson's "You Were Always on My Mind"—to his wife just before smothering her with a pillow. And the Harlem crackhead who killed his own sweet grandmother for 20 bucks. Another crazed killer was Daryl Holton, the Tennessee man who in 1997 executed his four children—during what was supposed to be a Christmas shopping trip—as a form of sick revenge against his ex-wife. A decade before that, in 1987, Gene Simmons, the Arkansas "hillbilly from hell", slaughtered 14 of his own kin after he was outed for incest. And in 2006 a twisted couple in Independence, Missouri, created a homemade snuff film as they sexually assaulted, tortured, and murdered a prostitute in their bedroom. I could go on, believe me.

But Daddy Daryl and Hillbilly Gene had nothing on these peace-and-love hippies. Their actions over three nights in Los Angeles 50 years ago are as depraved, debauched, and vile as any you will ever find. You can say this about professional killers: They do their work efficiently, typically with firearms. But there was nothing clean or clinical about the Manson murders. The perpetrators slowly slaughtered most of their victims with knives, swords, and bayonets. Their pitiable victims were given no consideration, let alone mercy, and the killers' own descriptions of the crimes at the time of their arrests are devoid of shame.

Gentle Buddhist Geek

Defense attorney Marvin Part, during a recorded debriefing, asked Leslie Van Houten: "Why in the world would you want to go out and kill somebody?" Here was her reply:

> *Because it had to be done. It had to be done just in order for the whole thing to be completed, for the whole world's karma to be completed, we had to do this. And I wanted to do it, because I thought that if I could go out and kill someone that I would—you know, it's not an easy thing to do it—and that I, in a sense, I would be giving up totally to what I believed in because I would have to pay the consequences if they were to come back.*

I'm not sure I fully understand what that word salad means, and I don't imagine Van Houten did either. Like most members of the Manson kill teams, she managed to find regret—and, cynically enough, God—only after it became clear that she stood no chance of freedom unless she did. I don't know how she and the others lived with themselves for even a day—an hour, a minute— after what they put this tossed-together assortment of luckless people through. These change-the-world hippies, who sang of love, proved to be soulless, murderous automatons.

Gary Hinman had the good instincts to turn down an invitation to join the Family—at least in part because he didn't want to hand over his possessions. But at age 34 Hinman was older and more worldly than Manson's acolytes. He and Manson were born six weeks apart in 1934, though the similarities end there. Manson, who yapped nonstop, was an undereducated but intuitive man who had learned the art of flimflam in reform schools and prisons, whereas Hinman was a geeky, quiet intellectual with a wispy Van Dyke and a premature combover. He dabbled in drugs, like most of L.A., and had become a college degree-collector. A native of Denver, where his parents operated a construction business, Hinman was a classical piano prodigy and the sort of kid who could play any instrument he picked up— guitars, horns, even bagpipes. He moved to L.A. to attend UCLA but chose an academic path unrelated to music. After earning a degree in chemistry, he then turned to the study of sociology, eventually entering a Ph.D. program at the same school. As with many grad students, the slog toward completing his thesis was long and slow, and college became a permanent state for him.

He moonlighted as a music teacher, instructing students on multiple instruments at a West Los Angeles studio, and owned a two-story, cedar-sided home in Topanga Canyon, 6 miles (10 km) up from the Spiral Staircase flophouse. Hinman became acquainted with various Family members through the interlaced commune scene in the canyon. He had been friendly with Bobby Beausoleil since 1967, and had given guitar lessons to both Manson and Beausoleil. Friends said he was a dedicated pacifist whose door was always open to hippies needing a place to lay their heads. Like many hippies (and some of the Beatles), Hinman was drawn to eastern mysticism. He had become a serious practitioner of Buddhism, and he was planning a religious pilgrimage to Japan— funded with a $1,050 travel gift from his Colorado father, Robert Hinman.

Arrival of Family Hit Squad

Four weeks after the Crowe shooting and financial score, when Manson was mulling over new cash targets, Hinman showed up in the Family's crosshairs. He had long been the subject of gossip about hidden wealth, apparently spread by Family member Ella Jo Bailey. After all, how does a professional grad student manage to own a 2,600 ft^2 (242 m^2) home? By one tale that ricocheted around the Family, Hinman had inherited $30,000. By another, he owned a portfolio of stocks that he held in negotiable securities. The Family recognized another sign of wealth in his driveway— three automobiles: a 1965 Fiat, a Volkswagen bus, and a vintage Thunderbird.

On Friday night, July 25, Manson dispatched a delegation to Hinman's home with instructions to convince the grad student by whatever means necessary to sign over his cars and surrender his wealth—the inheritance, the stocks, and cash on hand. The kill team that Manson selected was nauseating: Hinman's friend Beausoleil, backed up by two women he knew very well—Mary Brunner, Manson's original acolyte, and Susan Atkins. These were the two mothers of the Family, and they left behind their sons, ages 15 months and nine months, to help rob and murder a man who had been an important benefactor when Brunner's child was born. She feared that a social welfare agency would seize her baby—Manson's offspring—if case-workers learned of the living conditions at Spahn Ranch, so Hinman allowed her to use his home address as her official residence. He also donated formula, baby food, and clothing for the child.

Manson's delusion that Hinman would fork over his property failed immediately. The women knocked and entered at nearly midnight, and Beausoleil followed them inside when Atkins signaled from a window that their target was alone. Brunner later described the initial confrontation in a statement to investigators:

> *Then Bobby came up, and we just talked for a while, and then Bobby told Gary that we needed some money, and Gary said he didn't have any and then jabber-jabber, and then Bobby took the gun out, and said, "You know, we weren't kidding, we really do need some money," and then they got fighting over it, and Gary got hit with the gun.*

Jabber-jabber blah-blah-blah, and then her dear friend was left bloodied by a clubbing to the head. The shrugging dismissiveness of the ex-librarian's account is ice cold.

Slashed with Manson's Sword

Beausoleil and Hinman went around and around the kitchen, grappling for the gun, which went off at some point, although apparently no one was hit. Brunner said she and Atkins dodged from one corner to another to stay out of the way as the men fought. The team was flummoxed that Hinman was willing to fight for his life. Beausoleil handed the gun to Atkins and went to the living room to call Manson. Brunner said he reported: "Gary put up a fight, and things weren't going the way he wanted them to go."

Hinman, bleeding badly from his head, took the gun away from Atkins. (In Brunner's account: "He just like walked up to her and said, 'Now, Sadie, blah-blah-blah, cut this out. Stop acting this way.' And she backed off and he reached out and then wrested it away from her.") Beausoleil rushed back into the kitchen and recovered the gun after a four-way struggle. Twenty minutes after the phone call, at 1:30 Saturday morning, an irked Manson barged into Hinman's house with another follower, Bruce Davis.

In one of the most woeful details of this demented series of events, poor Hinman wailed for help when he heard the door open, hoping the visitor would rescue him. But Manson carried a sword, and Davis wielded a buck knife. As the kill team huddled in the kitchen, the new arrivals talked with Hinman in the living room, leading to what Brunner called a "scuffle." A cursing Manson stormed into the kitchen with a small cut to a finger. Meanwhile, Hinman wailed in the darkened living room. Manson had slashed him with the sword across the left side of his head, leaving a bloody gash 5 in (13 cm) long and a quarter-inch (6 mm) deep on his cheek. His left ear was sliced in half, from the midway point of the auricular cartilage right down to the aural canal. Both halves were still attached and bleeding. Years later, Beausoleil claimed that he asked Manson why he had cut their friend. "He said, 'To show you how to be a man.' His exact words," Beausoleil said. "I will never forget that."

Point of No Return

Manson and Davis drove off in Hinman's Fiat, leaving the mess to the overmatched kill team, who took turns guarding Hinman overnight. The next morning, Atkins and Brunner used a sewing needle and dental floss—the only filament at hand—to try to stitch together the ear, surely a case of the solution being more painful than the problem. Throughout the day on Saturday, Hinman alternated between chanting Buddhist mantras and trying to reason with the invaders.

"Please, we will forget it," he told them, according to Brunner. "We will call it a scratch. Just leave, get out of here."

Brunner said: "Well, we were kind of thinking, you know, Gary would heal up . . . We didn't even know what to do because we were afraid to leave the way he was, you know, because we knew he was going to charge us with assault. And we talked to him about him coming with us to the desert . . ."

Hinman showed them his checkbook, which had a balance of less than $100.

"We came for money," Brunner said, "but by this time it was obvious he didn't have any." The financial angle had become irrelevant to Beausoleil. "I knew . . . I'd end up going to prison," Beausoleil said. "Gary would tell on me, for sure, and he would tell on Charlie and everyone else. It was at that point I realized I had no way out."

In fact, there are always alternatives to murder. If Beausoleil had taken Hinman's advice, he and the women might have just faced assault charges.

If they had saved his life and given a full account of why they had targeted their friend, Manson might have been returned to his proper place in prison. The right decision likely would have changed the destiny of all the victims who would follow. But they took the wrong fork.

On Saturday evening, Beausoleil had another phone chat with Manson, who was stationed 15 miles (24 km) away at Spahn Ranch. "After he hung up," Brunner said, "he told me he was going to kill Gary that night."

Callous Murder of a Friend

As a prelude, Beausoleil directed Hinman to sign over the pink slip titles to his automobiles. Death came slowly to his friend. It was messy and merciless. Beausoleil confronted Hinman in a hallway and drove a knife blade nearly 2 in (5 cm) deep into the center of his chest.

The women listened from the kitchen as Hinman begged for his life. In another cruel twist, Brunner said Beausoleil tried to quiet Hinman by urging him to resume chanting as he lay dying on the living room floor.

In the meantime, the women wiped away their fingerprints and bagged up potential evidence, including their own bloody clothing. After some hours had passed and Hinman was still breathing, Beausoleil told Brunner he was going to "finish him off." He thrust the knife a second time into Hinman's chest, 2 in (5 cm) from the first wound. Brunner said Hinman was "in a coma" when Beausoleil stabbed him the second time, but in her account Atkins said the victim was very much alive. She heard him exclaim: "Oh, no, Bobby! Please don't! No more!"

Soon, Brunner said: "Gary started real loud deep breathing, real raspy, loud. He did it a couple times and Bobby . . . put a pillow over Gary's head for a while. Then he asked me to hold it there."

Imagine that scene: Brunner sat suffocating her friend and child's benefactor because they feared someone would be alerted by his loud death rattle. She was eventually spelled by Atkins, who was on pillow duty when Hinman expired. Atkins walked into the kitchen and said: "It's all over with." Police photos from the crime scene—shot after the body had been discovered and removed weeks later—show a large mat of clotted blood on the carpet beside a blood-stained pillow.

Following Manson's orders, the team used a towel to write "POLITICAL PIGGY" on a wall in Hinman's blood, and Beausoleil added a bloody cat's paw, intended to implicate the Black Panthers. After tidying up, Brunner reached into the dead man's pocket. They had arrived hoping for a $30,000 score, but the entire cash take was a $20 bill she lifted from his wallet, and loose change that Manson had taken. They called Spahn Ranch to ask for a ride back but were told they were on their own.

"There wasn't anybody that could come and pick us up," Brunner said.

They hotwired Hinman's red-and-white VW van (Manson had taken the keys when he stole the Fiat), then drove down the canyon road to a grocery store, where they discarded the bloody evidence in a dumpster. The three first-time killers then skipped happily into an adjacent café, where they used Hinman's 20 bucks to buy coffee and strawberry cake.

Everyone in the Manson clan had some idea their friend had been murdered.

As Lynette Fromme recounted in her memoir on the day after the murder as she was baking cinnamon rolls: "One of the

girls told me Gary Hinman was "floatin' in the cosmos." Fromme
was OK with that. As she wrote: "I chose not to ask questions."

Aftermath

At the close of Brunner's recorded confession four months later,
homicide detective Paul Whiteley gave her an opportunity to
blame the brains of this crime debacle. Whiteley said: "Now, stop
and think before you answer this one: Isn't it a fact that Charlie
Manson sent you people down to Gary Hinman's house?"

Brunner replied: "No, that is not a fact unless Charlie and
Bobby had some discussion before I got back from the ranch that
I don't know anything about, but Charlie never said anything to
me about going to Gary's house."

Facing the death penalty, Brunner eventually—but briefly
and reluctantly—turned against Manson. It took Beausoleil and
Atkins many years to fully acknowledge their roles in the atrocity.
"Gary was a friend," Beausoleil said decades later. "He didn't do
anything to deserve what happened to him, and I am responsible
for that."

In her memoir, Atkins belatedly admitted the monstrosity
of the murder—although she used passive language that allowed
her to stand at arm's length.

"The senseless, callous nature of this killing will never
cease to grieve and dumbfound me," she wrote. "In hindsight,
the death of Gary is perhaps the hardest thing to understand or
make sense of." Perhaps her memory was failing. What sense
could she possibly have made of any of the Family's homicides,
including those just a couple of weeks after Hinman's murder,
which would shower notoriety down upon them?

CHAPTER NINE

Mayhem on Cielo Drive

On Sunday, March 23, 1969, Charles Manson drove to Beverly Hills to visit a redwood-sided house at 10050 Cielo Drive, in Benedict Canyon, hoping to find record producer Terry Melcher, Doris Day's son and Dennis Wilson's buddy. Manson had been to the house the previous summer to meet with Melcher, and he was back yet again to try to convince the producer that he ought to get him a record deal. He found a party in progress but no sign of Melcher. He was intercepted outdoors by a guest who was spooked by the strange little hippie wandering around the property. Manson asked for Melcher but was told that the house was now rented by the movie director Roman Polanski and his wife, the actress Sharon Tate. Manson then slinked away, looking back over his shoulder.

Four and a half months later, he chose the Cielo Drive house to make his next big murderous statement. Charles (Tex) Watson described the seemingly spontaneous manner in which Manson announced plans for what would become America's most notorious home invasion. It came up suddenly during an everyday sexual bacchanal at Spahn Ranch. The only unusual thing about the evening was that the region was in the midst of a sharp, three-day heat wave that kept temperatures in the nineties, even at night:

> *We ate late that night, and sometime after dinner a lot of us were in the back ranch house with our clothes off, just lying around, some people making love. Usually these times were very mellow, all of us together like animals in a nest, nuzzling and warm, bodies close . . . Charlie sat up slowly and ran his finger across his throat. Then he told me to put on my clothes and come with*

him. As we walked up the hill in the darkness he said, "I've got a favor I want you to do for me tonight . . . but it'll take a lot of nerve to do it."

I told him he knew I'd do anything he wanted . . . He stopped and stared at me strangely [and said] . . . "I want you to go to that house where Melcher used to live. I want you to take a couple of the girls I'll send with you and go down there and totally destroy everyone in that house, as gruesome as you can. Make it a real nice murder, just as bad as you've ever seen. And get all their money."

Watson didn't blink, so Manson continued with his directive. He said he expected them to come back with at least $600—roughly the equivalent of $4,000 in today's money. Incredibly, he said they should pull door-to-door robberies in the neighborhood after the murders if they needed to top off their take to achieve the target of $600.

Manson told Watson to equip the team with ropes and knives, cut telephone wires to the house, wear dark colors, and carry a change of clothes. He handed him the .22 Buntline pistol—the gun he had used to shoot Lotsapoppa—but told him to opt for stabbing over shooting when possible. Gore was the goal, he emphasized—the murders should be so horrible that they would bring terror to Los Angeles. Quoting Manson, Watson wrote:

"Kill them all, mutilate them, pull out their eyes and hang them on the mirrors, and write messages on the walls in their blood." When he started listing what he wanted written—things

like HELTER SKELTER and RISE—I told him I couldn't remember all that. But he said it was okay; the girls would know what to write.

The Victims That Night

The lives awaiting the arrival of Manson's second kill team at 10050 Cielo Drive seemed ripped from the pages of an Agatha Christie novel. There was an altruist, Abigail Anne Folger, known to family and friends as "Gibbie." She was heir to the giant American company that made her surname synonymous with coffee in the U.S. (*"Folgers, mountain grown for better flavor."*) With her was an exotic foreigner, Folger's boyfriend Wojciech Frykowski, a Polish writer and recent émigré. Then there was a playboy, Jay Sebring, a native Alabamian who remade himself into Hollywood's hairstylist-to-the-stars. And, of course, there was Sharon Tate, the beautiful actress who gave a brand name and a glamorous headshot to the invasion. Finally, there was the forgotten outsider, Steven Parent, an unlucky teenager who happened to be on the property, trying to make a few bucks by selling a radio to the young caretaker.

Then as now, the Beautiful People of greater Los Angeles were sprinkled about over vast tracts of hilltop, canyon, and coastal neighborhoods. But the celebrity class is really a village unto itself, where everyone seems acquainted, if not friendly. The Benedict Canyon home, perched on a wooded hill overlooking Los Angeles, was an apt example. It was owned by Rudi Altobelli, a talent manager who had represented such A-list stars as Henry Fonda, Katharine Hepburn, Sally Kellerman, and Valerie

Harper. He rented his house for $1,200 a month—roughly $8,000 now—to an unbroken chain of celebrities. Terry Melcher and his girlfriend, the actress Candice Bergen, had moved out in February and yielded to Polanski and his newly pregnant wife. Their housewarming guests were said to have included Jane Fonda, Tony Curtis, Warren Beatty, and three-quarters of the Mamas & the Papas (minus Denny Doherty).

Abigail Folger

Although Abigail Folger was born to wealth and enjoyed an elaborate debutante ball, she was not a country club type. She grew up an artsy intellectual in San Francisco, and was a budding poet, painter, and pianist. After excelling at the Santa Catalina School, a Catholic boarding high school for girls in Monterey, she then moved to Boston to attend Radcliffe College, Harvard's female twin sister, where she was a musical theater star. She added a graduate degree in art history from Harvard, then worked at an art museum in Los Angeles and in publishing in New York.

In January 1968, the Polish writer Jerzy Kosiński introduced Folger to Frykowski, an old school friend from back home who had just arrived in the U.S. At 31 years old, Frykowski was said to be an aspiring writer—although he seemed to aspire more than write. He and Folger were soon a couple and a few months later they left New York for Los Angeles, moving into a house just off Mulholland Drive in Laurel Canyon. Still just 25 years old, Folger did not settle in among the idle rich. Like her mother, Ines, Folger was an earnest activist who followed the old Catholic dictum of tending to the less fortunate. Ines Folger donated time and money to the Haight-Ashbury Free

Medical Clinic in San Francisco, whose services were used by many in Manson's circle. To the surprise of no one who knew her, Abigail Folger went to work in the Watts ghetto as a volunteer social worker.

Folger and Frykowski became close friends with Tate and Polanski, another Pole, through their Laurel Canyon neighbor, Mama Cass Elliot. They met Jay Sebring, Tate's ex-boyfriend, through the same clique.

Jay Sebring

Sebring's story seems to have emerged in 12-point Courier font from a scriptwriter's IBM Selectric. He was born in 1933 in Birmingham, Alabama's gritty steel capital of the South, grew up in a Detroit suburb, served a stretch in the Navy just after World War II, and then landed in Los Angeles, where he upgraded his name from the meh John Kummer to the sleek Jay Sebring, inspired by the famous 12-hour Florida car race.

At the dawn of the Sixties, barbershops offered only a few assembly-line choices—a crew cut, a high-and-tight "regular," or, for the adventuresome, a quiff, each held in place with a double splash of hair tonic or a glob of pomade. Fresh off the boat and looking for a career, Sebring chose to attend beauty school—not barber college—and brought a mod sensibility to male coiffure. The "Sebring Look" soon had clients lined up out the door, paying ten times the going rate for a spin in a traditional barber chair. For that you got a wash, a layered cut, a style, and a blow-dry. The Rat Pack led the Hollywood conga line toward Sebring's scissors. He created a successful line of haircare products—Sebring International—and expanded his exclusive shops to other cities, places like New York and London, where men were willing to pay steeply for a periodic ear-raising.

Sebring was an undersized man with an oversized reputation as a lady-slaying Lothario. He buzzed around L.A. in Mustangs and Porsches, with one starlet after another riding shotgun, and his trophies included Tate, whom he began dating in 1964.

Sharon Tate

An ex-beauty queen from Texas, 26-year-old Tate had arrived in Hollywood five years earlier, appearing in commercials and TV bit parts, while studying acting and waiting for a break. Her film career was launched in 1967, when she was cast in a surf-movie sendup, *Don't Make Waves*, and as one of the fallen women in *Valley of the Dolls*. She also won a featured role that year in a vampire spoof, *The Fearless Vampire Killers*. While shooting that film on location in the Italian Alps, Tate fell in love with the young director, Polanski. She broke the news to Sebring in a phone call, and the movie-set couple married in London in January 1968.

The quality of her roles improved after the wedding. She had third billing in *The Wrecking Crew*, the last in a four-film series featuring Dean Martin as federal agent Matt Helm. She got pregnant late in 1968, but flew to Italy in March 1969 (days after Manson accidentally crashed her party) to shoot her final film, a comedy entitled *The 13 Chairs*. Tate had concealed the pregnancy from her husband, who had made it clear that he did not want children, but before flying home she belatedly broke the news to him. He was also working in Europe. Arriving back in Los Angeles on July 20—the night of the American moon

Polish film director Roman Polanski marries Sharon Tate at the Chelsea Register Office, 20 January 1968. The couple met in 1966 when Polanski cast Tate as the innkeeper's daughter in his comedy, The Fearless Vampire Killers.

landing—she returned to the Cielo Drive rental, where Abigail Folger and her boyfriend had been housesitting while the movie couple was working abroad. She asked them to stay until August 12, when Polanski was due home.

Manson's Kill Team

On Friday, August 8, Tate, Sebring, Folger, and Frykowski had dinner at El Coyote, the landmark Mexican restaurant on Beverly Boulevard in L.A., then reassembled at Cielo Drive. Abigail Folger retreated to a back bedroom to read, Frykowski fell asleep on the sofa, and Tate and Sebring chatted in the master bedroom. They had no way of knowing the horror that the night would hold.

Manson's kill team No. 2 was led by 23-year-old Charles Watson, the strapping former wig salesman from the Dallas area. He was accompanied by three women, including Susan Atkins, who had snuffed out Gary Hinman's life with a pillow two weeks earlier. (Mary Brunner, Atkins' female partner in the Hinman murder, was not available because she was in jail following her arrest for using a stolen credit card at a Sears store a day earlier.) The other two women selected for the Tate job were new to the craft. Twenty-one-year-old Patricia Krenwinkel, a diminutive native Angeleno, was the third to join Manson's harem in 1967, just after Brunner and Lynette Fromme. The final member of the team was 20-year-old Linda Kasabian, the hippie from Maine who had joined the Family just months before, with a toddler daughter on her hip. According to Family legend, Kasabian was selected because she was the only one available with a valid driver's license. She was assigned as wheelwoman for the getaway car, a tan 1959 Ford Galaxie sedan that Manson commandeered from a Spahn Ranch hand.

Wrong Place, Wrong Time

The team rolled up at the Tate house just after midnight, in the first few minutes of Saturday, August 9. They parked out of sight down the hill, and Kasabian was posted as lookout. Following Manson's directions, Watson shinnied up a utility pole and cut the telephone line to the house. As he, Atkins, and Krenwinkel pushed through a bushy embankment onto the property, they were startled to see headlights come around the house from the caretaker's cottage. Behind the wheel was Steven Parent, 18, a red-haired kid from suburban L.A. who was planning to start college in a month. Parent worked two jobs; as a plumbing supply delivery boy and as a salesman at a Wilshire Boulevard stereo shop. Just a week earlier, he had become acquainted with William Garretson, the young caretaker at Cielo Drive, after Parent picked him up hitchhiking and drove him home. Garretson invited him to stop by anytime, and he took him up on it that night, arriving at 11:45 to try to sell him a Sony Digimatic clock-radio. He wasn't interested, but they swigged a beer before Parent set out at 12:15.

Here's how Watson described their surprise meeting:

> *We had barely gotten over the gate when there was the sound of a car, and headlights loomed at the top of the driveway, heading toward us. I told the girls to get into the bushes, lie down, and be quiet. The driver of the car had to stop and roll down his window to push the button for the automatic gate, and as he did so I*

stepped forward out of the shadows, gun in right hand, knife in left, commanding him to halt.

A terrified teenage boy looked up at me, his glasses flashing . . . As I lunged forward, the boy cried out: "Please, please, don't hurt me. I'm your friend. I won't tell." I shot him four times [five, according to coroners] *and at some point struck out with the knife, slashing at the left arm he raised to shield his face. After he had slumped back across the seat I reached in the window, cutting the motor and lights before I pushed the car part of the way back up the driveway where it would be less visible . . .*

It's hard to understand, but no one beyond the kill team seemed to hear—or react to—those startling reports from the Buntline .22. Not caretaker Garretson, not any of the four people in the main house, and not a single neighbor there at the mountaintop terminus of a quiet dead-end street.

"You're All Going to Die"

Emboldened, the team moved toward the house. Watson cut a window screen into the foyer, and they were quickly inside. They first encountered Wojciech Frykowski, sleeping on a living room couch. He awoke to a gun barrel in his face. Watson growled: "Don't move or you're dead." He then directed Atkins to search the other rooms.

The ensuing events are best told in Atkins' remarkable words. She gave this account a few months after the murders, in an interview with L.A. defense attorneys Paul Caruso and Richard Caballero:

So I went down the hall to Abigail Folger's bedroom and Sharon Tate's bedroom . . . I went in Abigail Folger's room and she put her book down and looked at me, and I smiled and waved. And I looked in and saw Sharon Tate and the other younger man, the shorter man [Jay Sebring] . . . I came back out and I told Tex, "There's three more in there." And so he told me to take the rope and tie up [Frykowski] . . . And I was shaking so bad I couldn't tie his hands but I got the rope around and couldn't pull it tight. And he was so petrified he just laid there and didn't say a word. And he kept asking Tex, "What do you want? What do you want? Who are you?" And Tex said, "I'm the devil. I'm here to do the devil's business." And, "We want all your money. Where's your money?" . . .

And then Tex said, "Go in and get the other people and bring them out here." So I took my knife and I went in and stood by Abigail Folger's bed and said, "Go out in the living room, and don't ask any questions." And I went into Sharon Tate's room and told them to go out in the living room. And the three of them were pretty much terrified by what was going on.

Folger was dressed in a long white nightgown, and the very pregnant Tate wore a bra and panties, with a negligee draped over her shoulders.

Jay Sebring came into the living room and said, "What's going on?" and Tex said, "Go over and sit down." Jay Sebring proceeded to advance on Tex, and Tex shot him. And he fell on the floor . . . And Sharon went through a few changes [laughing], quite a few changes. . . . She said, "Oh my God, no." Miss Folger didn't say anything, she just stood there.

Watson and the women bound the injured Sebring and Tate together, then attached both of them to a rope they looped over a ceiling beam. Once everyone was subdued, Watson demanded their money, and someone came up with $72—short of Manson's $600 target. Atkins continued:

One of the ladies said, "What are you going to do with us?" and Tex said, "You're all going to die." And this caused immediate panic. And Tex told me to kill the big man, Frykowski. Well, I went over to him and I raised the knife and I hesitated. And as I hesitated, he reached up and grabbed my hair, he started pulling my hair. So I had to fight for my life as far as I was concerned. I still had the knife. Somehow he managed to turn my head. He was still holding my hair . . . and he was fighting and I was kicking him, and I proceeded to stab him three or four times in the leg. And then while this was going on, Abigail started getting loose and was fighting with Katie [Patricia Krenwinkel] . . .

    Well, as this went on there was a lot of confusion going on. I don't remember exactly what happened, but I remember seeing Frykowski going outside, and as he was going outside, he was yelling for his life, he was screaming really loud. And I said, "Tex, help me. Do something." Tex went over and hit him five or six times over the head with the butt of the gun [which] broke the gun handle. The gun wouldn't work anymore, and [he] proceeded to stab him. While he was stabbing the man was still screaming. I'm surprised nobody heard anything. And he was pretty much half dead on the porch. That's why all the blood was there, I imagine . . .

Sharon was starting to get herself loose from the rope, and the Folger girl had already broken loose and was fighting with Katie, and I was just standing there watching. There wasn't much I could do . . . I went over and got Sharon and put her in a head lock. She didn't fight me, I just held her. Then she was begging me to let her go so she could have her baby, and Katie was calling for me to help her because Folger was bigger than Katie and Katie had long, long hair. She was pulling on Katie's hair, and Katie was calling for me to help her. So I called to Tex to do something. Tex came back into the house and reached up to stab Folger and she looked at him and said, "You've got me. I give up." And Tex stabbed her and she was on the floor. I think he stabbed her in the stomach because I saw her grab down here. And then Tex went back outside because the other man, Frykowski, had gone outside and was on the lawn by then, still running and calling for help, and he proceeded to continue killing him . . .

Death of a Sixties Icon

This left Sharon Tate as the sole occupant of the house who was not dead or dying. Atkins said Tate asked to sit down, so she led her to the couch. The actress tried to appeal to Atkins' feminine sensibilities, but her efforts were wasted, even though Atkins had given birth to a son ten months earlier. Atkins had no empathy, like most sociopaths.

"She said all I want to do is have my baby," Atkins said, "and I knew I had to say something to her before she got hysterical."

So what she said was this: "Woman, I have no mercy for you."
She continued her story for the attorneys:

> *Then Tex came back in and said, "Kill her. Katie said to kill her."*
> *I reached to grab ahold of her arms. I didn't want to kill her, so I*
> *grabbed ahold of her arms and said, "Tex, I can't kill her. I've got*
> *her arms. You do it." And Katie couldn't kill her. So Tex stabbed*
> *her in the heart and he told us to get out . . . When Tex came out*
> *. . . he said, "Sadie, go back and write something on the door." . . .*
> *I didn't want to go back into that house but something made me*
> *go back in the house, and I got the towel that I had tied the man's*
> *hands with and I went over to Sharon Tate and I flashed, Wow,*
> *there's a living being in there. I want it, but I couldn't bring*
> *myself to cut her open and take the baby. I knew it was living. I*
> *knew it wouldn't live.*

For the second time in two weeks, Atkins witnessed the gruesome
sound of death. Caruso asked whether Tate was bleeding much.

"Yes," she replied, "and I could hear the blood inside her
body gurgling. It was the same sound I'd heard with Hinman."

"That's the death rattle," Caruso said.

"Is that what they call it?" Atkins said. "It's not a very
pretty sound." Yet she was able to set aside her disgust to do
Manson's bidding. "I reached down and turned my head away
and touched her chest to get some blood and proceeded to go
to the door," she said. "And the only thing I remember being
instructed to write on the door was 'Pig,' so I proceeded to take
my hand and write 'Pig' with the towel and threw the towel
back and ran outside."

A policeman stands in front of a car containing the sheet-covered corpse of Steven Parent, one of the five victims at the barn-style home of actress Sharon Tate in Benedict Canyon. The bodies of coffee heiress Abigail Folger and Wojciech Frykowski were found on a lawn next to the trees that can be seen at the far left.

Back at the Ranch

The team rendezvoused with Kasabian and drove back toward Spahn Ranch, ignoring Manson's $600 mandate. They stopped at a random house to rinse off the blood with an outdoor hose and were confronted by the homeowners. They then pulled into a service station to gas up the car, using the minimal proceeds from the murders. Watson described their arrival back at the ranch:

> *Charlie was waiting for us on the boardwalk of the old movie set, dancing around naked with Nancy Pitman in the moonlight. His first words were, "What're you doing home so early?"*
>
> *I told him what had happened—it had been messy, like he wanted, lots of panic, everybody dead. Sadie told him my line about the devil, and he grinned, pleased . . . Then he looked each of us in the eye solemnly.*
>
> *"Do you have any remorse?" he demanded. "No," we each replied.*
>
> *"Okay," he said gently. "Go to sleep and don't tell anyone."*

As the women walked away, Manson called Watson back, looked up at him, and asked: "Was it really Helter Skelter?"

"Yes," Watson replied, "it was sure Helter Skelter."

Frenzied Stabbings

Indeed it was. In fact, Atkins' account, as gruesome as it was, badly understated the extent of the knifework. Thomas Noguchi, L.A.'s chief medical examiner, led a team of pathologists in cataloging the wounds, an inch-by-inch examination that created a scorecard of sociopathy. Noguchi found that Sharon Tate had been stabbed not just once, as Atkins suggested, but 16 times in the back and chest. Many of the knife thrusts had resulted in deep wounds to the heart and lungs. One-third of the blows would have been fatal on their own, Noguchi said.

Sharon Tate's dear friend Jay Sebring had been shot once and stabbed seven times. He bled to death. Abigail Folger had suffered 28 savage stab wounds. Her boyfriend, Frykowski, put up a mighty fight. He was shot twice, clubbed with the gun butt a dozen times, and stabbed an incomprehensible 51 times. Each victim suffered a long, slow death. In her account, Atkins had suggested that Watson did most of the stabbing, minimizing her involvement and Krenwinkel's. That was dishonest. Watson did not inflict more than 100 stab wounds on his own.

Driving Home to Their Deaths

The next night brought even more grotesque violence. If Manson's concept was to induce terror by the sheer randomness of his victims, he could not have found a more perfect pair than Leno and Rosemary LaBianca. They lived at 3301 Waverly Drive, an upscale home in L.A.'s Los Feliz section, in the rising hills below the famed Griffith Park Observatory. Leno, the son of a successful wholesale grocer, grew up in Los Angeles. He married his high school sweetheart, did an Army hitch in Europe, then followed his father into the family business when he returned home from the war. He and his wife, Alice, separated in 1955 and divorced in 1959, after parenting three children. Leno then began dating Rosemary Struthers, a fellow recent divorcee with children who worked as a waitress at the Los Feliz Inn. Late in 1959, they drove to Las Vegas for a quickie wedding.

Leno LaBianca had grown weary of the grocery business, so he sold his stake and dedicated his time and money to his true passion, thoroughbred horseracing. His entrepreneurial new wife picked up the financial slack by opening a successful dress and gift shop on busy South Figueroa Street. After several moves over the course of their marriage, in 1968 the LaBiancas bought the Waverly Drive house from Leno's mother. It was a homecoming; he had grown up there as a teenager in the 1940s.

But the couple had a difficult time settling in. Presciently, something about the house spooked them. They believed that someone was breaking in when they were gone. Objects in the house would be moved around, and they would come home to find their dogs in the yard after leaving them indoors. They reported their suspicions to the police, but an investigation went nowhere. In May 1969, Rosemary wrote to her stepdaughter: "We haven't had any more robberies, but every time I come home I expect to either find someone in the house or something missing. I think the police have stopped working on the case . . ."

Forty-four-year-old Leno and 38-year-old Rosemary took a long drive in their green Ford Thunderbird on Saturday, August 9, to visit her 15-year-old son Frank. He was vacationing with the family of his friend Jim Saffie at Lake Isabella, in the Sierra Nevada range 150 miles (240 km) north of L.A. When they returned home at 1 a.m. on Sunday, Rosemary retired to the master bedroom while Leno stayed in the living room, obsessing over *Daily Racing Form* charts for Sunday's thoroughbred races.

Charles Manson decided to take a more active role in the second night of Helter Skelter. Although he had ordered Charles Watson to make the Tate murders "as gruesome as you can," he was disappointed at the kill team's inefficiencies in getting the job done—too much screaming and chasing. "I'll have to show you how to do it," he said.

Orders Killings Then Leaves

They set out in a crowded car as darkness fell on that Saturday night. The expanded team included all four participants from 24 hours earlier—Watson, Atkins, Krenwinkel, and Kasabian—as well as Manson, Leslie Van Houten, and Steve (Clem) Grogan, the purported dimwit. They spent several hours driving around Los Angeles, as Manson directed Kasabian from one neighborhood to the next, searching for a soft target. He stopped several times to case a possible location but rejected each one. As with the Tate invasion, he ultimately chose a place that was familiar to him, like a squirrel returning to a buried nut. A year earlier, Manson and other Family members had attended a house party on Waverly Drive in Los Feliz. He guided Kasabian there, then creepy-crawled the vicinity before choosing the place next door, 3301 Waverly Drive, home of the LaBiancas.

Manson and Watson crept up a steep driveway to the Spanish Revival home and peered through the windows to find Leno dozing in the living room. They broke in, woke Leno at gunpoint, then bound and gagged him, covering his head with a pillow. Manson assured the man that they were robbers who intended no harm as long as he kept quiet and cooperated. The intruders then went to the bedroom and gave Rosemary the same treatment and story.

Manson scrounged up what cash and coins he could find—again, the take was petty—and went out to the car. He then ordered

Krenwinkel and Van Houten to go in and help Watson kill the couple and, once again, scrawl messages in blood. After that, he drove off with Atkins, Grogan, and Kasabian, leaving the other three behind to commit murder and manage their own getaway.

This was another demonstration of Manson's cynicism and his followers' naivety, similar to the Hinman murder, when he slashed the man's face, then left the dirty work (and the getaway) to the kill team's own devices. Manson did the prep work with the LaBiancas—the *mise en place* of murder—then scurried off, leaving the actual butchery to his seconds. How could it have not occurred to Watson, Krenwinkel, and Van Houten that they were being used? Nonetheless, the two female automatons rendezvoused with Watson inside. Here is Watson's account of what happened, beginning with his exchange with the women concerning Manson's marching orders:

I thought I was whispering when I asked, "Did he say to kill them?" Perhaps my voice was louder than I thought, because as they nodded grimly, Leno LaBianca began to scream from the living room, "You're going to kill us, aren't you? You're going to kill us!"

I somehow knew from the look on her face that Leslie didn't want to go through with what was coming, but, like all the rest of us, she must have felt she owed it to Charlie to do whatever he asked, since he'd given himself so totally for us. Katie [Krenwinkel], on the other hand, began to look through the kitchen drawers for knives with positive relish.

Mr. LaBianca continued to shout. I remember being surprised that he could talk so much with the wire and pillow

Enjoying her moment in the sun, star witness Linda Kasabian pictured at a press conference in Los Angeles after being granted immunity from prosecution.

material in his mouth. As the girls ran to the bedroom on my instructions, I walked back to the sofa with the bayonet and the horror began all over again. I drove the chrome-plated blade down full force. "Don't stab me anymore," he managed to scream, even though the first thrust had been through his throat. "I'm dead, I'm dead." The shiny bayonet plunged again and again . . .

As LaBianca rolled off the sofa onto the floor, I could hear his wife screaming from the bedroom: "What are you doing to my husband?" There were the sounds of some sort of scuffle, and I ran in to join the girls. Mrs. LaBianca was in a corner of the room, still hooded with the pillowcase, swinging a large lamp [the wire was wrapped around her head] in an arc that kept the two girls from getting close to her. The bayonet had greater range and I struck out time after time, even after the woman had fallen to the floor. Katie had run into the living room at some point, and now she returned, saying, "He's still alive!"

I went back to the living room and used the bayonet again, over and over. Suddenly Charlie's face clicked in my head, as I heard the words he had sent me off with the night before: "Make it as gruesome as you can." Out of some horrible part of my brain an image formed and I reached down and carved WAR on the bare belly below me. Later, while I was washing away the LaBiancas' blood in their own shower, Katie would add to the grotesque picture by stabbing the dead man 14 times [with an ivory-handled carving fork that she left wobbling in his stomach], *and by planting a small steak knife in his neck, both these weapons coming from the LaBiancas' kitchen drawers.*

After I'd finished my butchery on the man, I went back to the bedroom and told Leslie to help Katie stab the woman,

even though it was obvious that Rosemary LaBianca was already
dead. Leslie obeyed me, striking mainly on the exposed buttocks,
but with none of the enthusiasm that Katie showed . . .

Bloody Messages

In her own numbed account, Van Houten said: "Tex handed me
the knife and, you know, said, 'OK,' you know, 'Get to it.'" And
she did. In all, the three killers stabbed Rosemary LaBianca 41
times. As Watson showered, Krenwinkel and Van Houten used
the victims' blood to leave the calling-card messages: "DEATH
TO PIGS," "HEALTER SKELTER" (misspelled by Krenwinkel,
who was not the sharpest knife in the Family's cutlery drawer),
and "RISE." The latter was a reference to one of Manson's White
Album lyric obsessions, "You were only waiting for the moment
to arise," from Paul McCartney's "Blackbird."

Before they left, the kill team paused to raid the refrigerator,
snacking on cheese and milk while standing amid two fresh bodies
and bloodied walls. They also took a liking to the LaBiancas' pet
dog, which they had just orphaned. Susan Atkins later recalled a
conversation she had with Krenwinkel the next day. Krenwinkel
fondly mentioned the dog, of all things, as she was describing her
participation in the murders of two human beings.

"She said the dog just sat and watched the whole thing,"
Atkins said. "And the dog came up to them and wagged its tail,
and she reached down and patted it on its head."

How nice. After scarfing the dead couple's food, stealing
a bag of their coins that Manson had overlooked, and showing
kindness to their pet, the killers walked outside and were surprised

to find their ride was gone. Toting a satchel of bloody clothing, they wandered joylessly around Los Feliz—whose root meaning is Spanish for "happy."

They were lost, hoping to find their way at first light.

CHAPTER TEN

Crackpots and Flapping Lips

L ike hundreds of other black housekeepers on any day of the week in Los Angeles, Winifred Chapman left her apartment early on Saturday, August 9, for the long commute up into the hills to scrub the floors and clean the toilets of the Hollywood elite. She faced a 16-mile (26-km) city bus journey from her flat on 46th Street in South Central.

After a transfer, her second bus dropped her at North Canon Drive and Santa Monica Boulevard, two blocks from the gilded strip of Rodeo Drive. The final 3 miles (5 km) of her trip was a steep climb up Benedict Canyon to the narrow, winding Cielo Drive—Spanish for *sky*—where a cul-de-sac dead-ended at her destination. She normally took a taxi from the bus stop, but on that morning a motorist friend happened to be passing as she stepped off the bus, so she hitched a ride and saved a buck on cab fare.

Before even passing through the security gate at about 8:20 a.m., Chapman noticed the wire dangling from a pole outside the house. She picked up the morning newspaper, walked around back to the kitchen—her customary entrance—unlocked the door, and immediately checked a phone. Finding no dial tone, she hurried toward the front of the house—passing a room that Sharon Tate had begun remodeling as a nursery—to alert "Mrs. Polanski" to the phone problem.

"Since our electric was on, I surmised it was the telephone wires and started up front to awaken someone," she later told a grand jury.

"And then what did you notice?" a prosecutor asked.

"Well," she replied, "that is when I saw the bodies and the bloody clothes and what-have-you."

Chapman doubled back through the kitchen and ran screaming down the hill to the home of Ray Asin, who was greeted at his door by the frantic stranger who was unable to speak coherently but gasped a string of horrifying words: "murder . . . blood . . . bodies!" Police arrived and took the human inventory of the ghastly scene, which included the knifed bodies of Folger and Frykowski, 50 ft (15 m) apart out on the lawn; the teenager Parent, dead in his car and unrecognizable from point-blank gunshots to the face; and Sebring and Tate, lying dead on the floor but still linked together by a rope slung over a ceiling beam, leading investigators to surmise that they were threatened with hanging before they were stabbed to death.

Carving Fork Protrudes from Torso

Thirty-six hours later, as police were just beginning to dig in on the Cielo Drive investigation, Rosemary LaBianca's son, 15-year-old Frank Struthers, arrived home at 8:30 p.m. Sunday after his summer getaway to Lake Isabella. The teen was creeped out from the moment the father of his friend dropped him off at the house on Waverly Drive in Los Feliz, 11 miles (18 km) away from the Tate crime scene. Unusually, the shades in the house were drawn. When no one answered his knock, he walked four blocks to a pay phone on Hyperion Avenue and called his house. Getting no answer, he phoned his older sister, 21-year-old Suzanne Struthers. She and her boyfriend, Joe Dorgan, hurried over and accompanied Frank inside, where they found a crime scene no less horrible than that at 10050 Cielo Drive. Leno LaBianca's body was sprawled in the living room, a 12 in (30 cm), ivory-handled carving fork protruding from his torso—the handiwork of Patricia Krenwinkel.

Blood-ink messages were scrawled in block lettering on a wall and the refrigerator. There were two grace notes in the discovery: Suzanne Struthers had waited outside and was spared the visuals, and her brother and Dorgan backed out of the house before the teenager could find his mother's body in the bedroom. The three then ran to a neighboring house and alerted the authorities to the second murderous abomination of the weekend in Los Angeles.

Auditory Witnesses

The world was introduced to this "cultist-style murder spree" in hundreds of front-page newspaper stories over the ensuing days and weeks. Many were the work of Linda Deutsch, a young reporter with the Associated Press in Los Angeles, who would become known as American journalism's queen of celebrity crime. To Deutsch, common sense suggested a link between the Tate and the LaBianca murders. In a bulletin story on the AP national newswire on Monday, August 11, Deutsch reported on a manhunt for "a suspect in the bizarre killings of actress Sharon Tate and four others five miles [11, in fact] from where a couple was found slain later in a similar style." She reported that the Tate mansion caretaker, "slim, tousle-haired William Garretson," had been booked on suspicion of murder, then followed up a day later with news that he had been cleared.

Proximity made Garretson a suspect. In addition, the police were incredulous that he had failed to hear primal screams and gunshots that night. He explained that he was awake during the entire horror but was engrossed while writing letters and listening to music. But it turned out that there were earwitnesses, after all.

The nearest house, at 10070 Cielo Drive, was about 100 yards (91 m) from the Polanski–Tate home. Its occupants, art

Police guard the driveway of the LaBiancas' house on Waverly Drive, where Leno LaBianca, 44, and his wife Rosemary, 38, were stabbed to death. There were striking similarities with the Tate crime scene.

historian Seymour Kott and his wife, the painter Ethel Fisher, had just moved in from New York City weeks before. They went to bed at midnight, and Fisher nudged Kott awake sometime shortly thereafter, when she was startled by a series of three or four gunshots—the murder of Steven Parent, apparently. After listening intently, but hearing nothing further, the couple went back to sleep.

Another auditory witness was more proactive. Although it's 3 miles (5 km) away by car, the Westlake School for Girls is barely 2,000 ft (610 m) down the ridge from the Tate property. On the night of the murders, Tim Ireland was supervising an overnight camp-out there for three dozen children. At 12:40 a.m., he heard a man scream in the distance, seemingly begging for his life: "Oh, God, no! Please don't!" The exclamation ended suddenly. Ireland checked on his campers' well-being and reported the scream to his supervisor. Convinced that someone's life was in danger, he took the additional step of driving around the neighborhood but did not find his way to Cielo Drive, where he might have been able to save a life or two.

Crackpot Theories

As calendar pages turned without an arrest, some interlopers began pushing crackpot theories about the case. In one strange example, the writer Truman Capote—basking in the fame of *In Cold Blood*—told host Johnny Carson on *The Tonight Show* that he believed a lone killer, "a very young, enraged paranoid," was responsible for the Tate murders.

Meanwhile, two other flimsy predispositions related to the murders became set like concrete. First, the Los Angeles Police

Department stubbornly refused to admit what seemed obvious: that the Tate and LaBianca murders were committed by the same people. Inspector K.J. McCauley told the press: "I don't see any connection between this murder and the others. They're too widely removed. I just don't see any connection."

He made the comments while standing outside the LaBianca home, which, even in the worst L.A. traffic of 1969, was only a 30-minute drive away via Sunset Boulevard from the Tate place. The LAPD seemed determined to prove Inspector McCauley right, no matter the cost.

The second assumption, which showed up in "enterprise" news stories following up on the murders, was that Sharon Tate and her friends somehow had it coming because of an immoral Hollywood lifestyle. Many stories focused on drugs or alleged marital discord between Tate and Polanski. On the day he was dismissed as a suspect, young Garretson stood with his lawyer before a group of reporters.

The attorney, Barry Tarlow, said that, at the request of police, he would not allow his client to talk about "sex or drugs" at the Tate mansion. In the next breath, Tarlow acerbically added that he was certain "sex and drugs" were pivotal to the murders. He added: "I think there is a maniac running around."

Another far-out example, published by the *Los Angeles Times* a week after the murder, said one of the victims, "Polish playboy" Wojciech Frykowski, "was the principal target and was executed because of his deep involvement with narcotics distributors." The questionable story had one source, an unnamed Polish immigrant "informant." The story managed to besmirch his wealthy girl-friend, Abigail Folger, as well: "The informant told officers that

Frykowski was a cocaine user and that Miss Folger was in love with him and supplied him with money for his drug habit."

To be fair, the police encouraged that narrative with an investigative report that said of Frykowski: "He had no means of support and lived off Folger's fortune . . . He used cocaine, mescaline, LSD, marijuana, hashish in large amounts . . . Narcotic parties were the order of the day." According to an often-repeated true crime legend, Folger's parents used their wealth to stifle "salacious gossip" about Abigail, but any official documentation of such an effort—including court records—is lacking.

Blame-the-Victim Reporting

Perhaps most remarkable among the blame-the-victim reporting was a story published by *The New York Times* three weeks after the murders:

> *Polanskis Were at Center of a Rootless Way of Life;*
> *4 Slayings Illuminate International Milieu of Movie Makers.*

Here was reporter Steven V. Roberts' declamation, delivered with the sort of moralizing normally found in froth-and-scum tabloids, not the high-collared "Gray Lady":

> *The murders remain unsolved, and in the absence of facts, amateur detectives are having a field day. But the savage killings did more than provide local cocktail party chatter.*
> *The murders brought into focus several life cycles— disparate yet connected—that displayed some of the glamour and intrigue that have long fed the Hollywood script mill . . .*

The Polanskis . . . had been near the center of a loose group of film makers who were described with all the current clichés: mod, hip, swinging, trendy.

This group was not only more youthful but also more international than the Hollywood Establishment. Its members were "rootless vagabonds," as one studio executive put it, at home in a dozen places, and yet belonging nowhere. Their names never appeared on the maps tourists buy on Hollywood Boulevard to find the homes of the stars; they had no homes.

The swinging jet-set theme was central to red carpet-style reporting at the victims' funerals, where Tinseltown attendees were highlighted in bold face: Peter Sellers, Yul Brynner, Warren Beatty, Kirk Douglas, James Coburn, Steve McQueen, Paul Newman. *Newsweek* advanced *The Times'* celebrity bacchanal story in a follow-up article that even more explicitly stretched to link kinky sex to bloody murder:

The bizarre murder of actress Sharon Tate and four others at Polish film director Roman Polanski's secluded villa in the Hollywood hills confronted the police with a fascinating whodunit. But nearly as enchanting as the mystery was the glimpse the murders yielded into the swinging Hollywood subculture in which the cast of characters played. All week long the Hollywood gossip about the case was of drugs, mysticism and offbeat sex—and, for once, there may be more truth than fantasy in the flashy talk of the town.

Or maybe not.

Mourners at Sharon Tate's funeral included her sister, her mother Gwendolyn Tate and husband Roman Polanski. Their naked grief contrasts with the many salacious newspaper reports of the murders.

Decomposed Corpse Found

By the time these unfortunate stories were published, the LAPD might have already had the Manson Family in its sights if it hadn't been paralyzed by internecine law enforcement conflicts with the LASD—the Los Angeles County Sheriff's Department, viewed by city cops as a rival agency, not an ally.

On the evening of July 31, a week before the twin "cultist" murders, friends of Gary Hinman went to check on him at his Topanga Canyon house. He hadn't been seen for nearly a week, and the usually reliable music teacher had failed to show up for a series of scheduled lessons with students. The friends, Mike Irwin, John Nicks, and Glenn Giardinelli, first noticed that Hinman's Fiat station wagon and VW van were missing from his parking area. When they climbed the steps to his front door, they were repelled by a deathly odor. The men then retreated to a neighboring house and called the sheriff's office, which had jurisdiction outside the L.A. city limits. Deputy Paul Piet described the ghastly scene in his official report:

We observed numerous flies around the southeast window . . . On entering living room, we observed victim lying on his back with his head pointing west and his body east. Victim had a blanket covering his body and a pillow partially covering the left side of his face. Victim was observed to be in a decomposed condition, face blackened with maggots on and around the head area. We observed splotches of blood on the blanket in the area of victim's chest.

World's Dumbest Criminal?

Another week along, at 11 a.m. on August 6, Trooper Forrest Humphrey of the California Highway Patrol stopped to check on a white 1965 Fiat wagon that was parked on the shoulder of northbound Highway 101 near San Luis Obispo, 200 miles (320 km) from Los Angeles. Humphrey thought the car was unoccupied, and was surprised when a head popped out of a sleeping bag in the rear. It was Bobby Beausoleil, proving once again—as a homicide sergeant often reminded me early in my reporting career—that "intelligence is not a prerequisite to the perpetration of a criminal act." He was sleeping in his murder victim's car on a busy, heavily patrolled highway—along an infamously long and steep incline up to the Cuesta Peak summit of the Santa Lucia Mountains. Beausoleil drowsily explained that the car had broken down on the climb, which was not unusual on the Cuesta grade. He showed its paperwork, including Hinman's pink slip, and Trooper Humphrey did his job, checking the tag and registration. When he learned that the car had been reported stolen by the L.A. County Sheriff, Beausoleil was quickly in handcuffs. Later that day, Detective Sergeant Paul Whiteley questioned Beausoleil. This was his summary:

> *Undersigned proceeded to the San Luis Obispo County Jail and interviewed suspect. After advising suspect of his Constitutional rights, which were waived, suspect stated on 7–25–69 he hitchhiked to victim's home in the accompaniment of two females; that upon his arrival victim had been cut across the left side of his face and stated he had been jumped by Negros. Further, that he attempted to sew up victim's ear with a needle and thread and*

stayed with the victim until 7–26–69 at which time victim gave him the keys to the Fiat and the pink slip which he signed so that suspect would have no trouble with the law. Further, that he could use the car indefinitely. Suspect stated he left victim lying in the living room on the floor dressed as he was found by the original responding deputies.

Whiteley surely suppressed a laugh. Beausoleil, a new nominee for world's dumbest criminal, was charged with murder.

Police Rivalry Slows Investigation

As a lead investigator on the Hinman homicide, Sergeant Whiteley had puzzled over the bloody scrawl on the walls inside Hinman's home—"POLITICAL PIGGY" and the cat's paw. He had never seen anything like it at a crime scene, so his ears pricked up when he learned that similar blood-ink messages had been left at the Tate and LaBianca scenes as well. How could it be a coincidence that "PIG" was smeared at Tate's and "DEATH TO PIGS" at the LaBiancas'? Three pigs seemed like a solid trend to the investigator.

On August 10, even before the LaBianca murders were discovered, Whiteley contacted Sergeant Jess Buckles, an LAPD detective working the Tate case. Whiteley briefed Buckles on the Hinman details, including the promising "pig" connection and the use of knives in both cases, and what's more he told Buckles he had a suspect in custody, readily available for interrogation. But Buckles blew him off as an interloper from the county. As Whiteley later recounted, his LAPD counterpart said: "Naw, we know what's behind these murders. They're part of a big dope transaction."

When Whiteley suggested that it wouldn't hurt to talk to Beausoleil, Buckles gave him a figurative pat on the head. "If you don't hear from us, that means we're on to something else," he said. Buckles then kept the tip to himself, failing to report it to anyone that mattered—like his boss.

These sorts of conspicuous missteps in the Manson investigation have provided fodder and fertilizer for a fervent club of conspiracy theorists who believe mysterious unseen forces connived to shield the Family. My reading is that the delay in arrests resulted from law enforcement incompetence, not a secret cabal. But in retrospect, it does seem as though the police went to extreme lengths to ignore the obvious.

On Sunday, August 17, page two of the local news section of the *Los Angeles Times* might have given the police a crime-solving roadmap if only they had been paying attention. The lead story on the page, at the top right, was a long, week-later regurgitation of the essential facts of the Tate case. (The story was written by Dial Torgerson, a rising-star *Times* reporter who 14 years later was killed by a grenade while covering the Sandinista War in Nicaragua.) Immediately below that story was an eight-paragraph report on the funerals of Leno and Rosemary LaBianca. And just to the left, in a coincidence of newspaper layout that seems impossible, was a story with this headline:

> *Police Raid Ranch,*
> *Arrest 26 Suspects*
> *In Auto Theft Ring.*

The story explained that the group—11 men and 15 women—"was stealing Volkswagens, dismantling them and converting them into dune buggies." The suspects had been "living like animals," it was reported, including four women and four infants who "were found sleeping on the floor of a dirty, broken-down trailer."

Spahn Ranch Raid

The August 16 raid was an all-hands operation for the sheriff's office. More than 100 deputies descended on Spahn Ranch at 6 a.m., catching the Manson Family in repose. The lawmen seemed to enjoy the job. As another story reported: "Most of those arrested were women, some of whom were nude and some wearing only bikini bottoms, deputies said." The long list of those arrested included Charles Manson, Lynette Fromme, and Susan Atkins, although she appeared in the blotter under her alias, Sadie Mae Glutz. Police said they confiscated seven rifles and two handguns, but the Family was reunited after just a few days. Everyone was released without charges due to an administrative glitch: the search warrant had the wrong date. Nonetheless, a dragnet was closing in—for the car thefts, not the murders.

The raid gave Manson a new score to settle. He believed that Donald (Shorty) Shea, the ranch hand and part-time western movie stunt man, had snitched to the police about the Spahn Ranch chop shop.

"Once out of jail," Susan Atkins later explained, "the first order of the day for Charles Manson was retribution . . . Whether Donald Shea actually had anything to do with the police raid or not has never been proved. . . . What's important was that Manson thought Shea was responsible for the raid."

Two weeks later, on about August 28, Manson and an all-male kill team took Shea for a ride to the far reaches of the ranch. The group included Manson, Charles Watson, Steve Grogan and Bruce Davis. With Shea sitting in the front seat, Grogan clocked him from behind with a pipe wrench. The big man was then dumped out of the vehicle, stabbed to death, and buried. His body would lie undiscovered for eight years.

Death Valley Raids

The sheriff's raid had freshly soured George Spahn on the Family, so Manson and his followers retreated to Goler Wash in Death Valley and their squats at the adjacent Myers and Barker ranches. But their reputation followed them. On October 10, 1969, the Barker property was raided by a task force that included National Park rangers, California Highway Patrol officers, and Inyo County deputy sheriffs. The Family was suspected, once again, of stealing dune buggies as well as setting fire to expensive earthmoving machinery. Manson was absent for the Barker raid, but he was arrested when the authorities returned two days later and searched the Myers property. They found him hiding in a kitchen cupboard. The police had interrupted a Family dinner of Sugar Pops cereal, caramel corn, and candy bars; their diet was getting worse as their imagined Armageddon approached. Manson was booked on suspicion of arson and receiving stolen property and was ordered to be held on $25,000 bail. He would never again walk as a free man.

These raids, the second and third on the Family in just four weeks, began to kill the buzz that serial murder had not. "That this period is nothing like the love-filled days in San Francisco or the first year in Los Angeles goes without saying," Atkins wrote. "That the atmosphere is still anything like communal is ridiculous."

Family Members Flee

The rats began to abandon the sinking ship. Patricia Krenwinkel fled to her mother's home in Mobile, Alabama, Charles Watson scurried back to his Texas hometown, and Linda Kasabian made her way back east to New York. Of the ten people arrested in October, most were quickly released, including Family mainstays like Lynette Fromme, Catherine (Gypsy) Share, Sandra Good, and Leslie Van Houten.

Manson was an exception, and so was Susan Atkins. She was held on bail because a biker associate of the Family had told the police that she knew something about a homicide case involving a sliced ear: Gary Hinman.

As Shakespeare wrote in *Hamlet*: "Murder, though it have no tongue, will speak with most miraculous organ." That is often because perpetrators of this godlike act, the snuffing of another human being's life flame, can't help but flap their lips about their wondrous feat. And so it was with lusty, loud-mouthed Susan Atkins.

CHAPTER ELEVEN

Sadie and the Snitches

Susan Atkins was transferred from a local jail in the desert hinterlands to the Sybil Brand Institute, the vast women's lockup in a county public safety complex in East Los Angeles. By coincidence, she was assigned to a bed in an open dormitory that was adjacent to the cot of Veronica (Ronni) Howard, a prostitute who was serving a sentence for using a forged prescription to obtain drugs.

Atkins, Howard, and a third inmate, prostitute Virginia Graham, became friendly over the course of several weeks spent sleeping in close proximity.

The women may or may not have had a sexual relationship, although Atkins put her own spin on that in her memoir. She wrote:

> *I elicited the unwanted attention of two middle-aged career criminals, Virginia Graham and Ronni Howard* [they were 37 and 33, respectively; Atkins was 21], *who apparently decided they were attracted to me. In order to avoid them, I began talking about the biggest news on the television—the killing of Sharon Tate.*

Imagine the wonder on the faces of Graham and Howard: this criminal ingénue had landed in their laps and was blabbing a story that would become their tickets out of jail. In mid-November, about six weeks after Atkins was arrested, the two women told jail personnel that they had information on the Tate murders, and Sybil Brand supervisors contacted the LAPD. After a preliminary debriefing on November 23, two homicide division detective sergeants, Mike McGann and Frank Patchett, returned to Sybil Brand two days later to record interviews with the informants.

Few Details Spared

Atkins had spared few details in her account of the murders and dynamics of the Manson Family, providing a basic narrative outline that Vincent Bugliosi would use in his prosecution. Ronni Howard made notes after their conversations, and she referred to them in her interview with the detectives. Here are some excerpts:

> She said, "You remember this Tate deal?" And I said, "Yeah." . . . She said, "Well, they'll never find out who did these murders." . . . I said, "I don't believe you did it and you're just talking big, you know. Anyone can say they did it." And she said, "Oh, no." And she went on to tell me that there were four of them that went into the house . . . She said they parked the car on the street and they walked up to the house. She said they picked the house because it was secluded and out of the way. She said first they cut the wires . . . The young fella was leaving in the car . . . and asked them, "Hey, what are you doing here?" and Charlie [Watson] shot him. I forget she said two, three, or four times, but I know that it was more than once. But she said the stereo was going so the people in the house didn't even hear when the fella outside was shot. And they went into the house . . . She said that all the girls had knives and Charlie had a gun . . . I think she said one fella was sleeping on the couch and she said he was really surprised . . . She said that Sharon Tate . . . was in the bedroom. . . . She said that Sharon just said, "Well,

why are you doing this, you know, don't kill me, let me live just
for my baby," and Sadie said, "I got no feelings for you, bitch.
We're doing you a favor. We're releasing you from this earth."
And she said she had no feelings whatsoever for her because . . .
you don't really live until you die.

Sergeant McGann asked Howard whether Atkins had admitted
to stabbing Tate or other victims. She replied: "Oh yeah, because
she even told me, 'Well, it felt so good . . . the first time that
I stabbed her.'" Howard said Atkins "got all enthused" while
describing the feel of burying a knife in human tissue. "It felt like
going into nothing—just like into air," Atkins said.

Mainly through Atkins, Howard had acquired a deep
understanding of the Family's genesis and plans: the connection
to the Beach Boys and Terry Melcher; their theft of Volkswagens
for dune buggy conversions; the fever dream to wait out a Helter
Skelter apocalypse at the "devil's hole" in the desert; the scrawling
of variations of "pig" at each murder scene to implicate the Black
Panthers; and on and on. Atkins seemed delighted that she could
shock her jailhouse roommates.

Howard recounted sexual bon mots that Atkins shared,
including a much different take on who was romancing whom
in jail:

See, the sight of blood excites her, and, like she said, it is like
a sexual release. She says it is even better than a climax, you
know, and by stabbing somebody like she said, after the first
time it gets good to you . . . [It also] excites her to have somebody

scream. She said it just sends a rush all the way through her, you know . . .

Sergeant Patchett: What else did she talk about besides these murders? You say she mentioned her kid now and then?

Howard: Yeah, how she used to masturbate him, make him get a hard on, a little one, I forget how old, seventeen months or something, she said.

Patchett: She did that to the boy?

Howard: Yeah, imagine . . .

[Howard was then asked a question about "morals and scruples" in the Family]

Howard: She said if you feel like making love to this one or that one or five or six or whatever, you know. Evidently this Charlie, he was something of a man, you know. She said that, you know, maybe five or six girls and Charlie all at one time. She said if she felt like making love to a girl she would just tell her and that is why she said she couldn't understand why they didn't do it in jail, you know. And I said, "Well, you know, you have to conform according to where you are," and she said, "Yeah, well I keep forgetting because I don't have any inhibitions at all."

Patchett: Do you think she is a lesbian?

Howard: No. She isn't really a lesbian. She just likes whatever, whether it's in the form of a male or female.

Patchett: Did she ever make a pass at you?

Howard: No, not really. She just told me, she said, "Hey, I would like to make it with you one time." I told her, I said, "Well, hey, you have to conform to where we are."

I didn't want to scare her off so she wouldn't tell me anything else.

Aimed to Feign Insanity

Howard said Atkins described Charles Manson as "the devil sometimes, and other times he is Jesus Christ." She said she believed that Manson was able to control her mind and that of several other female followers. I'm not sure that it was due to mind control, but Atkins clearly was a Manson supplicant. In speaking to the women in jail, Atkins aped many of Manson's hillbilly platitudes, including that racial segregation was natural and that women were made to serve men. Howard explained: "She said she will do anything that a man tells her to do because that is why women are put on this earth—to do what a man tells you to do, no matter what it is."

Manson had schooled his acolytes to feign insanity should they be arrested, just as he planned to do. Atkins discussed that, too, with Ronni Howard and Virginia Graham.

"Even if they do convict her, she said that they will probably send her to a mental institution," Howard said. "She said, 'I'll make those psychiatrists think that I'm crazy . . . I want to make them think I'm insane.'"

Howard added wryly: "I was thinking to myself, she really is insane."

Family Members Arrested

About a week later, news leaked that a "nomadic band of hippies" had emerged as leading suspects in the series of murders in Los Angeles. Patricia Krenwinkel, Charles Watson, and Linda Kasabian, three of the Family members that Atkins had identified to her jail pals, had been quietly arrested on murder warrants in Alabama, Texas, and New Hampshire.

On December 1, Susan Atkins was allowed to leave the Sybil Brand Institute temporarily to meet with two lawyers, Paul Caruso and Richard Caballero, at Caruso's office in Beverly Hills. She retold for them the same unburnished narrative she had shared with Howard and Graham. That evening, the attorneys leaked some of the details to the *Los Angeles Times*. The next morning, Charles Manson got his long-awaited star turn in the United States. The *Times* story began:

> *Charles M. Manson, accused in the mountain-desert area of rustling four-wheel-drive vehicles, has emerged as a key figure in the investigation of the killings of Sharon Tate and seven others in Los Angeles.*
>
> *The bushy-haired, wild-bearded little man with piercing brown eyes has been tabbed the leader of a hippie-type roving band whose members call him "God" and "Satan"—and now two attorneys say clan members killed the actress and others.*

Susan Atkins, already charged in the murder of Gary Hinman, retold her story once again on December 5, before a Los Angeles County grand jury. As she began, prosecutor Vincent Bugliosi asked whether she understood the concept of self-incrimination.

She said she did—but didn't really care. "I understand this, and my life doesn't mean that much to me," Atkins said. Its value had not yet bottomed out.

CHAPTER TWELVE

On Display

The Vincent Bugliosi-led grand jury in Los Angeles heard from 22 witnesses over two days, including the teenage Family member Dianne Lake and Susan Atkins, who embodied her "Sexy Sadie" nickname by testifying in a mini-dress. Additional testimony came from an unusual source, Danny DeCarlo, a member of the San Fernando Valley chapter of the Straight Satans, a California outlaw motorcycle club. DeCarlo and a few other Satans had begun hanging around the Spahn Ranch in 1968, enjoying an occasional sex romp on the saloon floor. Manson thought the bikers could come in handy for protection during the looming apocalypse, and DeCarlo became a de facto Family member. That fall, at about the time Susan Atkins was blabbing to her jailmates, DeCarlo approached the LAPD with his own incrimination of the Family.

It took just 20 minutes of deliberation for the grand jurors to recommend charges. On December 8, 1969, four months after the Tate and LaBianca murders, Atkins, Charles Watson, Patricia Krenwinkel, Leslie Van Houten, and Linda Kasabian were indicted for the slayings.

Manson Gets the Fame He Craved

But top billing among the accused killers went to Charles Milles Manson.

"Manson had played the part of an evil Pied Piper for almost two years, leading a changing band of restless young men—and particularly young women—from San Francisco's Haight-Ashbury to a handsome Pacific pad to an abandoned western movie location to Goler Wash [in the desert]," Jack V. Fox wrote for United Press International. "In the end, some had turned against the man they called 'Jesus.'"

Susan Atkins leaves the grand jury room after testifying against Charles Manson. She embodied her "Sexy Sadie" nickname by giving evidence in a mini-dress.

Another national wire story called him "the high priest of a weird hippie cult."

At last, Manson had found a route to the fame he craved. Writers from *Rolling Stone* wanted to meet him—albeit to profile an accused mass murder mastermind, not a musician. The attention scratched the itch of his piggish ego. In a series of court appearances and media interviews after his arrest, Manson performed the routine he had been practicing for three years on Mary Brunner, Lynette Fromme, and their gullible playmates.

As with all dictators, Manson was accustomed to speaking without interruption in sermons to his Family. He tried to stipulate those same terms in court and in interviews—and he usually got his way. In one of his first press sit-downs—at the L.A. County Men's Central Jail, with Michael Hannon of the *Los Angeles Free Press*—Manson lectured the journalist "about the advisability of my quoting him directly" instead of paraphrasing. Like many interviewers, Hannon ceded control to his subject—a mistake for any journalist. He sat back and listened to what he described as a speech by Manson. It was well-rehearsed: An outcast crawls out from underfoot briefly to better himself but is stomped down again by The Man:

> *You want to know where my philosophy comes from? I'll tell you. I'm not from your society. I have spent most of my life in a world of bars and solitary confinement. My philosophy comes from underneath the boots and sticks and clubs they beat people with who come from the wrong side of the tracks. People like me are society's scapegoats. They keep getting away with it because no one will say anything.*

"I don't have any guilt," proclaimed Charles Manson at a brief press conference following a hearing where it was decided to continue proceedings in the Gary Hinman murder case.

I have been in jail 22 years. My body has been locked up but my mind is free. When I get outside on the street, I see all kinds of people whose bodies are free, but their minds are all locked up.

Killer's Love of Life

Just as he did with his followers, Manson used his prison props and woebegone backstory to seduce journalists. Hannon fell under Manson's spell, arguing in the first of a series of articles that Manson deserved the opportunity to be released on bail since "the possibility certainly remains that he may in fact be wrongfully accused." He went a step further in a follow-up, writing of Manson: "He is simply a dramatic example of the unreasonable and oftentimes sadistic exercise of power by the law enforcement bureaucracy over those in its clutches." He was accused in nine murders, but Hannon treated Manson as a victim, just as he had hoped.

Hannon wasn't alone, particularly among the counterculture press. *Rolling Stone*'s Dalton wrote that he arrived for his own jailhouse interview with Manson believing that he was innocent—a patsy suspect plucked from the hippie culture. But Dalton was certain of Manson's guilt by the time he left the jail that same day, and that was reflected in his *RS* cover story, published on June 24, 1970, under the headline: "Charles Manson: The Incredible Story of the Most Dangerous Man Alive."

In another early interview, Manson spoke by phone from jail to Steve Alexander, a writer for *Tuesday's Child*, a short-lived L.A. underground newspaper. The call was more soliloquy than conversation. A transcript suggests that Alexander asked just three or four questions (unfortunately including, "What's your birth sign?"). As usual, Manson did all the talking, punching the replay button on the story of his life—and his love of love.

I'm from Juvenile Hall. I'm from the line of people nobody wants. I'm from the street. I'm from the alley. Mainly I'm from solitary confinement. You spend twenty years in institutions and you forget what the free world is. You don't know how the free world works. And then you come out and you live in it and you say, "Wow, I've been locked up for twenty years but my mind has been free." And I come outside and I see everybody's got their minds locked up and their bodies are free . . .

So when I got out I met a 16-year-old boy. I was living in Berkeley, and I asked him where he lived. And he said, "Well, I live out in my sleeping bag." I said, "Well, don't you work?" and he told me, "Hell, no. Nobody works. You don't have to work." I said, "Well how do you eat?" He said, "Well I eat at the Diggers [a Haight-Ashbury charity]." And I said, "Well how can you live that way?" He said, "Come on." He put his arm around me like I was his brother, and he showed me love . . .

He took me to Haight-Ashbury and we slept in the park in sleeping bags, and we lived on the streets, and my hair got a little longer and I started playing music, and people liked my music, and people smiled at me and put their arms around me and hugged me. I didn't know how to act. It just took me away, it grabbed me up, man, that there was people that are real. You know, I just didn't think there were such real people . . . It was the young people walking up and down the street trading shirts with each other and throwing flowers and being happy, and I just fell in love. I love everything . . .

So I got a school bus and I asked anybody, "Anybody wants to go can go in the school bus." . . . And we all turned our minds off and we just went around looking for a place to get away from The Man . . . And like it was just a trip, we were going nowhere, coming from nowhere and just grooving on the road because the road seemed to be the only place where you can be free when you're moving from one spot to another . . .

And then we went out and got out in the desert. We found a whole world out in the desert . . . And we walked around for weeks, following the animals and just seeing what they do. And there is a lot of love there. That's where most of the love is, in the young people and in the animals. And that's where my love is . . . If you love everything, you don't have to think about things—you just love it. Whatever circumstances are handed to you, whatever a dealer deals you, whatever hand you get handed, you just love the hand you got, you know, and make it the best you can. And that's what I've always thought. I've never had much schooling. No mother, no father. In and out of orphanages and foster homes. And then to boy's school and reform schools. Like it's always been like . . . my head is empty.

Much of Manson's public jabbering in the months and years that followed was contrived nonsense, following through on his frequent advice to his acolytes to feign insanity if arrested. To me, his comments to Alexander are the best summary I have found in the vast Manson archive of how he was feeling about himself and his life at that moment. He honestly seemed to believe that love had helped him triumph over his challenging origins.

And now consider that this was a man facing at least seven counts of murder, and that conviction likely would lead to a date in California's gas chamber. Yet in his psychopathic mind, Manson was succeeding in his post-prison design for living. To paraphrase Ronni Howard, Susan Atkins' jail snitch, maybe he really was crazy.

Street-Corner Vigil

To that point, I marvel 50 years later at the spectacle created by Manson, his female co-defendants, and the tight circle of women who clung to him to the bitter end and beyond. Facing charges that threatened their very existence, Atkins, Krenwinkel, and Van Houten all but skipped down courthouse hallways in their jail dresses, on some days holding hands and singing the lyrics of co-defendant Manson's songs. (The fifth defendant, Charles Watson, was fighting extradition from Texas and would later face trial alone, which is why he escaped the torrid notoriety of the others.)

Outside the Hall of Justice in downtown Los Angeles, Manson's women held vigil at the corner of West Temple Street and North Broadway, where they often sat cross-legged surrounded by reporters, tourists, and rubberneckers. The group regularly included Family stalwarts Mary Brunner, Nancy Pitman, and Sandra Good, and they were frequently joined by Kathy Gillies and Kathryn Lutesinger. Like their accused-murderer sisters inside the courthouse, the street-corner women sometimes sang Manson tunes, and they worked with needle and thread on an elaborately embroidered vest they had been sewing for Manson for months. They vowed to return every day until Manson was released—"and he will be released," Good often added. In one remarkable episode, the five women sat on a bench outside a grand jury room displaying a hand-drawn sign that read: "Judas Day: A snitch in time . . ."

Snitching became a central theme of the Manson Family murder and conspiracy trial, a predictable circus that began with jury selection on June 15, 1970. Linda Drouin Kasabian, the young mother from Maine who served as getaway driver for the Tate and LaBianca murders, was granted immunity from prosecution in exchange for her testimony against the accused killers.

On the first day of testimony, July 24, Manson walked into court with an X carved squarely between his eyes—a symbol, he said, of his *persona non grata* status as an outcast American. Playing monkey see/monkey do, Atkins, Krenwinkel, and Van Houten each bore their own etched X in the next court session. So did their Siren sisters out on Temple Street.

String of Witnesses

Slowly and methodically, prosecutor Bugliosi used testimony from ex-Family members and others to build a framework to support his narrative about Manson's stranger-than-fiction "Helter Skelter" motive. Kasabian was a powerful witness, giving brief but precise answers about events before, during, and after the murders. (She was indefatigable, spending 18 days on the witness stand.) Her testimony was key in linking Manson directly to the murder conspiracy since she was party to his directions. Dianne Lake and Paul Watkins, the young stoner musician who turned against Manson soon after the murders began, testified to Manson's complete control over the commune members. Watkins explained Manson's vision of "Helter Skelter":

> *There would be some atrocious murders . . . Some of the spades from Watts would come up into the Bel-Air and Beverly Hills District and just really wipe some people out, just cut bodies up and smear blood and write things on the wall in blood, and cut little boys up and make the parents watch. All kinds of just super-atrocious crimes that really would make the white man mad.*

Bugliosi called 84 witnesses and introduced nearly 300 pieces of evidence before wrapping up his case on November 16, five months after the proceedings had begun. Manson's side chose to call no witnesses, a common tactic in U.S. jury trials when the defense feels that the prosecution has failed to convince jurors of guilt. In this case, the defense attorneys had a second motivation: They knew that the women and Manson wanted to testify, but they were apprehensive about what they might say. The female defendants—including Atkins, who had recanted her tell-all grand jury testimony—desperately wanted to declare from the witness stand that Manson was not responsible for the murders. Their attorneys were dead-set against it.

Court Rant

After a contentious sit-down with the principals, Judge Charles Older came up with a very unusual compromise: He would allow Manson to take the witness stand and speak extemporaneously out of earshot of the jury. Manson spoke for more than an hour, riffing as usual on his humble roots. His most salient comment about the charges he faced was this: "I have killed no one, and I have ordered no one to be killed." But he brought up snitching over and over as part of a misogynist rant aimed at Kasabian:

I have one law, and I learned it when I was a kid in reform school. It's don't snitch. And I have never snitched . . . You take Linda Kasabian and you put her on the witness stand and she testifies against her father [meaning Manson]. *She never has liked her father, and she has always projected her wrong off to the man-figure. So, consequently, it is the man's fault again, and the woman turns around and she blames it on the man. The man made her do it. The man put her up to it. The man works for her, the man slaves for her, the man does everything for her, and she lays around the house and she tells him what he should do . . .*

She got immunity on seven counts of murder. I don't know how much money she is going to make in magazines and things. You set her up to be a hero, and that is your woman. That is the thing that you worship. You have lost sight of God. You sing your songs to woman. You put woman in front of man. Woman is not God. Woman is but a reflection of her man, supposedly . . . You set this woman up here to testify against me. And she tells you a sad story. How she has only taken every narcotic that is possible to take. How she has only stolen, lied, cheated and done everything that you have got there in that book. But it is okay. She is telling the truth now. She wouldn't have any ulterior motive like immunity for seven counts of murder. And then, comical as it may seem, you look at me, and you say, "You threatened to kill a person if they snitch." Well, that is the law

where I am from. Where I am from, if you snitch, you leave
yourself open to be killed. I could never snitch because I wouldn't
want someone to kill me.

Following his deeply etched template, Manson veered into his
reflection/projection riff, which he used to slough off blame for
anything he did. "It is your creation," he said. "I never created
your world, you created it." In the next breath, he swelled with
machismo. "I am the beast," he said. "I am the biggest beast
walking the face of the earth. I kill everything that moves. As a
man, as a human, I take responsibility for that."

Sentencing Drama

As the trial drew to a close, few careful observers could have
disagreed with Manson's self-analysis. On January 25, 1971, the
jury declared Manson, Atkins, Krenwinkel, and Van Houten
guilty on all counts, including first-degree murder. The women
finally got their chance to speak during the sentencing phase, but
they wasted an opportunity to plead for their own lives. Instead,
they argued for Manson's innocence, parroting a cockamamie
story that the Tate and LaBianca murders were devised—by
Linda Kasabian, of course—as a cover-up for Gary Hinman's
murder. Manson showed up in court with his head shaved one
day, and his followers inside and outside the courtroom did their
own self-barbering, with buzzes or pixie cuts.

The jury had just two sentencing options—life in prison
or condemnation to the gas chamber. They announced their
decision after eight hours of deliberation on March 29, 1971. The
defendants "came into court giggling and smirking," according

Near the courthouse where the Manson trial was taking place, followers of Charles Manson show their solidarity through shaven heads and crosses carved into their foreheads. Manson had said, "I am the Devil and the Devil always has a bald head."

to a UPI account, and Manson launched a proactive attack on the jury. "You have no authority over me," he cried. "Half of you aren't as good as I am." Judge Older ordered him removed from the courtroom before the sentence was revealed. The women began their own screaming when they learned the jury's sentencing recommendation: Death. Atkins borrowed Manson's projection theme.

"You've judged yourselves," she shouted. She too was removed when she lunged at the jury box. Krenwinkel seemed to threaten the jury, saying: "You're removing yourselves from the face of the earth. You're all fools. There never has been any justice in this courtroom." And Van Houten chimed in: "Your system is just a game in which you all make money."

Manson was 36 years old on the day of his condemnation, Krenwinkel was 23, Atkins 22, and Van Houten 21. Defense attorney Paul Fitzgerald later said of the trial: "I fail to see how it solved anything. The society that kills its problem children denies itself." But jurors believed the outcome was just. "Charles Manson is a dangerous influence on society," said one of the 12, retiree Marie Mesmer. "I think I can go home with peace of mind now, knowing I have protected society."

In a poignant comment to a reporter after sentencing, Edward Atkins, Susan's father, seemed flummoxed by what his daughter had become.

"I loved her," he said. "I still do. She once did some very beautiful things. But that was a long time ago. I don't know what went wrong. I guess I never will."

CHAPTER THIRTEEN

"Absolute Respect"

History suggests that it takes humility, fortitude, or a sentence of life in prison without possibility of parole to prompt certain people to admit that they were wrong. Gradually, most of Manson's followers came around to the hard truth that they had been manipulated by a psychopath—most, but not all.

After Manson's arrest, two young filmmakers, Robert Hendrickson and Laurence Merrick, shot hours of 16mm footage in a series of visits to Spahn Ranch, where they interviewed Family members. The stars were Sandra Good and Lynette Fromme, the two acolytes who would hold Manson to their bosoms long after all others had come to their senses and pushed away the creepy little man. Good and Fromme performed for the camera—and *in absentia* for Manson.

In carefully staged scenes shot by the filmmakers in a barn (available on YouTube, like dozens of other Manson clips), Good, Fromme, and Nancy Pitman can be seen cradling pump shotguns and gripping buck knives. Fromme caresses her gun and says: "You have to make love with it. You have to know it. You have to know every part of it." She wore a wry grin: She knew it was a put-on.

In another scene, they sit beside one another on a wooden table, wearing short shorts and denim vests with fur collars, like armed lionesses. Good seemed to be in a trance, peering deeply into the camera and peacocking her machisma in a series of statements intended to shock.

"Whatever is necessary to do, you do it," Good says icily. "When somebody needs to be killed, there's no wrong. You do it. And then you move on. And you pick up a child and you move him to the desert. You pick up as many children as you can, and you kill whoever gets in your way. This is us."

Fromme chimes in: "Anybody that has ever gone against us—or anybody that would ever step in front of us—will be taken care of."

From off-camera, Merrick asks the women: "If you had to kill more, you'd kill more?" Good nods, and Fromme says: "Whatever we have to do . . . We leave our mind open."

Merrick asks: "And you may get an impulse and go out and kill tomorrow?" Good replies: "If it was right."

Merrick asks the women whether they were "worried about the police." Good replies by singing a bit of "Come and Get It," a contemporary hit song (written by Paul McCartney) for the Welsh band Badfinger: "If you want it, here it is, come and get it." A grinning Fromme adds: "But you better hurry 'cuz it won't be here long, you motherfuckers."

Deluded to the End

In another scene, Good crosses over into her own psychopathy. "What's the big deal?" she says. "Five or six people get killed, and you all freak out and put it on us. We're just reflecting you back at yourself." Good was still miming Manson's favorite projection/reflection tropes two decades later, when she described him in a 1990 TV interview as "a mirror—a reflection of yourself." In the same interview, she said of the mass murderer: "I have absolute respect for him."

I gather from the bizarre role-playing on camera at Spahn Ranch that Good and Fromme regretted they had been left out of the murder assignments. Perhaps Manson was protecting them. Among his followers, Fromme had always been regarded—with a degree of envy and resentment—as Manson's favorite. And Good was seen as the most blindly dedicated Manson robot. As far as

I can tell, neither woman has ever turned against their beloved muse. Fromme ended her admiring memoir about Manson with a pointed quote out of one of his letters from prison: "I've no thoughts of defeat. Unaware, I never gave up, never surrendered. I can be broken and dead but to lose is impossible because you cannot destroy the universe."

She wrote defensively about Bugliosi and "Helter Skelter," particularly the science fiction of their search for an underground fountain of youth. It was all quite rational, she claimed, as the Family tried to "do what was needed to survive." And that meant killing nine people—in addition to various other felonies, including theft and financial fraud—in their doe-eyed devotion to Manson.

Steep Cost of a Helter Skelter Ride

Few among Manson's followers walked away from their experience unscarred. Those who testified as prosecution witnesses, including Paul Watkins, Dianne Lake, and Linda Kasabian, were threatened, harassed, and cast out by the faithful.

The cost was steep for those who had a role in the murders, although their lives were spared when California suspended capital punishment in 1972 and commuted their sentences to life in prison. Among the other trials related to the murders:

- *Bobby Beausoleil was among those who had a death sentence commuted to life in prison. Convicted of Gary Hinman's murder in April 1970, he has been denied parole nearly 20 times since 1978. He went into prison at age 22 and nearly 50 years along, as 2019 dawned, he was one of California's longest-tenured senior inmates.*

- *After fighting extradition from Texas for more than a year, Charles Watson was eventually returned to California to face his comeuppance. Watson was the most prolific of the Manson killers, having had a hand in all five of the Tate mansion murders as well as those of Leno and Rosemary LaBianca. He too was convicted, sentenced to die, and saved by capital punishment commutation. Like Beausoleil, by 2019 Watson had lived behind bars for half a century, having been denied parole repeatedly since 1976. And following the path taken by a number of the other Manson convicts, he professed to a religious conversion in prison.*

- *Bruce Davis is one of the lesser-known Manson followers, having escaped much of the attention focused on the women. A native of Louisiana, he met Manson in the early days of the commune. Davis helped Manson slice Gary Hinman's ear in half, and he also participated in the murder of Donald (Shorty) Shea, the ranch hand killed in retribution for the dune buggy police raid. He was convicted of both murders and was sent to prison for life. Another prison preacher and model inmate, Davis was recommended for release by the California parole authority in 2017—but this was overruled by Governor Jerry Brown, who took a stern position on the Manson convicts, whom he blames for "some of the most notorious and brutal killings in California's history." (Like Davis, Leslie Van Houten, convicted in the LaBianca case, has been recommended for parole but this too has been denied by Governor Brown.)*

- *Manson and Steve (Clem) Grogan were also convicted of the Shea murder. Grogan was the rare Manson murder participant to win parole, largely because he had a bargaining chip. In 1977, he agreed to help the authorities locate Shea's body, which had lain undiscovered for years on a Spahn Ranch hillside. In consideration of his tip, he was paroled in 1985.*

The One Who Got Away

Lynette Fromme, Sandra Good, and Mary Brunner were all late additions to Manson's convicted felons' club. It is challenging to choose which of their crimes was the most mad; each was crazy in its own special way.

Brunner had a special standing in the Family as Manson's first acolyte and the mother of his son, Pooh Bear. By refusing to testify against him and the others, she was central to Manson's strategy to keep followers in the fold after his arrest. Good and Brunner were not implicated in the Tate and LaBianca murders because both were in jail at the time. They had been arrested for using stolen credit cards on August 8, the day before the Tate murders, at a Sears store 15 minutes from Spahn Ranch.

But Brunner had participated in the horrific slaying of Hinman, her friend and benefactor, and she immediately wavered when she was charged with murder in that case, along with Beausoleil, Susan Atkins, Manson, and Bruce Davis. Having studied for three years at the knee of a master manipulator, she crafted some manipulations of her own.

She showed that her true allegiance was to Manson alone when, in exchange for immunity from prosecution, she agreed to testify only against Beausoleil and Atkins. But her testimony over the course of two trials was a hot mess, as she first blamed

Beausoleil then recanted. In the end, Atkins and Beausoleil were convicted in spite of Brunner's sketchy evidence. Because of her immunity, Brunner escaped prosecution, even though she had tried to suffocate Hinman with a pillow, and many believe she got away with murder.

Airliner Hijacking Plan

Brunner's antic testimony won her an open door back into the Family, where she began plotting on behalf of Manson and the other Tate–LaBianca defendants. The grand plan was to hijack a commercial airliner and threaten to kill the passengers one by one until Manson and the others were released. It fell apart at the first step. On August 21, 1971, five months after Manson's conviction, Brunner, Catherine Share, and four men descended on a Western Surplus Store, a retailer of outdoor gear and military supplies, in the Los Angeles suburb of Hawthorne. They held customers and employees at gunpoint, then rounded up 143 rifles. Tipped by a silent alarm, police arrived and blocked their getaway, exchanging dozens of shots with the robbers, all of whom were soon in custody. Convicted of multiple felonies, Brunner and Share were sentenced to 20 years in prison but won early release—Share in 1975, Brunner in 1977.

Presidential Assassination Attempt

Share, another of the born-again-Christian Manson followers, became an anti-cult activist and Brunner returned to the Midwest, took a new identity, and fell into obscurity. She is the only key Manson figure who has never explained her actions through a memoir or a detailed interview.

Lynette Fromme (and her irresistible nickname, Squeaky) had her front-page turn in September 1975. Fromme and Sandra Good were living together in an attic apartment on P Street in the California capital of Sacramento. They had based themselves there because they wanted to be near Manson, who was incarcerated 25 miles (40 km) away at Folsom State Prison—even though neither was allowed to visit him.

By then, Fromme and Good had pivoted away from violent apocalyptic motivations toward violent environmental motivations. They had taken new names—"Red" and "Blue"—to indicate fealty to nature apparently. Fromme learned that President Gerald Ford would be visiting Sacramento on September 5 on political business. Dressed in a long red gown, she was waiting at 10 a.m. in a large but linear crowd as the president made the walk from his suite at the Senator Hotel across L Street to the State Capitol, for a meeting with California's newly elected 37-year-old governor, Jerry Brown.

As Ford approached, Fromme drew a pistol, pointed it at the president's midsection, and squeezed the trigger. She heard nothing but a metallic click, because she had neglected to chamber a cartridge—a violation of her gun porn film segment in which she declared that one must know one's weapons intimately. Secret Service Agent Larry Buendorf snatched the gun from her grip and took her to the ground. As she was being handcuffed, cameras caught her saying, "It didn't go off," as though that absolved her.

Fromme was convicted of the president's attempted murder and sentenced to life in prison, but was paroled in 2009. She does not address the Ford case in her memoir—in the same way, she fails to deal with the Family murders. The only mention of the

Ford incident is in the brief biography at the book's end, which reads in full:

> *Lynette Fromme spent thirty-four years in prison after pointing a 1911 model Colt .45 pistol at the President of the United States in order to get her imprisoned friends back in a courtroom. There was no bullet in the chamber of the gun.*

Now that is a writer grasping to control her narrative.

50-Year Prison Club

After the assassination attempt, police searched the Sacramento apartment that Fromme shared with Good and Susan Murphy, a neophyte Manson follower who had been drawn into Fromme and Good's bizarre house of mirrors. Authorities found evidence that the women had sent form-letter death threats to nearly 200 corporate executives, whom they accused of creating pollution. Good was convicted of federal charges and served ten years in prison, but that didn't change her estimation of Charles Manson. In the same 1990 interview in which Good declared "absolute respect" for Manson, she added that he ought to be removed from prison and installed as a leader of the United Nations, "in a position where he could put order back into this country." She managed no sympathy for his murder victims, but said of the prosecution of her hero: "From the very beginning, the cards were totally stacked against him."

As 2018 ended, Leslie Van Houten and Patricia Krenwinkel were still imprisoned, joining Charles Watson, Bobby Beausoleil, and Bruce Davis as soon-to-be members of the 50-year prison

San Quentin Prison in Marin County on the San Francisco Bay, where Manson was once imprisoned.

club. (Susan Atkins' incarceration proved terminal: She died of brain cancer in a prison hospital in 2009.) Davis was the oldest of the still-imprisoned group, at age 76, and Van Houten the youngest, at 69. Krenwinkel spent her 49th consecutive birthday behind bars on December 3, 2018.

"What I am today is not what I was at 19," Krenwinkel told *The New York Times* in a 2017 prison interview.

Her parole hearings have been an interesting study in how someone like her is caught forever in a web she spun for herself. Parole commissioners (and perhaps everyone else in the world) want a simple answer to this question: What motivated you to commit these abominable acts? And Krenwinkel, while expressing deep and no doubt heartfelt regret, has replied over and over, in one way or another, that she did it to please Manson. That answer does not suffice, as California parole commissioner Susan Melanson tried to explain to Krenwinkel in 2011:

> *This panel still finds it very hard to believe that an individual can participate in these crimes, the level of violence in these crimes, and not be able to identify something besides "I wanted him to love me" as the internal drive for participating. And that really continues to bother the panel today.*

Manson's Enduring Appeal

If this clutch of elder inmates is ever released, they will find that their old haunts are long gone. The Spiral Staircase hippie flop in Topanga Canyon was demolished long ago, and a wildfire destroyed most of the buildings at Spahn Ranch in September

1970, as the Manson trial was being held. Spahn died in 1974, and his old property is now part of a California state park.

Two things remained true of Charles Manson right to his bitter end.

First, despite spending 70 years of his life locked up, he was an incorrigible inmate unwilling to follow even the most basic rules. His final parole hearings, which he stopped attending, featured long catalogs of his rule violations—"literally too many to count," according to one state report. They ran the gamut from refusing work assignments, counseling appointments, and classes to destruction of prison property and grooming violations. Of course, Manson had nothing to lose because he knew he had no hope of parole. He saved his manipulation skills for other purposes.

Which leads to the second truth: Manson never lost his allure as a subject of enduring fascination. The case—in static, resolved status for five decades—is nonetheless avidly spy-glassed by an amateur detective corps of many, many thousands of people, something on the scale of the horde obsessed with the John F. Kennedy assassination.

I think it reflects the true crime fad that has overtaken cable television. The writer David Dalton told me he believes there may be more interest today in the gore than there was in 1969. "This grotesque, morbid stuff is part of our mass culture now," he said. "Every popular movie, every TV show seems to involve gore—zombies, skin peeling off, horrible wounds and injuries that we must see in vivid, close-up, high definition. He's probably popular with this same class since his murders were classic examples of violent fantasies. In his case, he actually did that. He had people go out and kill with knives and swords."

Would-Be Bridegroom

Likewise, Manson has never lost his appeal among certain women. His mail was heavy with come-on letters, some no doubt inspired by the previously discussed hybristophilia, a sexual attraction to dangerous men. Manson would answer some of his correspondence in loopy, childlike script often containing enigmatic metaphors, like this one from 2011: "Cowards are like chickens in the barn yard. The horse kicks off on the dogs—dogs get feared and snap at the chickens, chickens peck off on each other. Last chicken gets bloody and pecked to death."

In 2007, Manson began a visitors'-room relationship with Afton (Star) Burton, a 19-year-old woman who had moved 2,000 miles (3,200 km) from Illinois to Corcoran, California, to be near his prison. She told *Rolling Stone* in 2013: "I'll tell you straight up, Charlie and I are going to get married. When that will be, we don't know. But I take it very seriously. Charlie is my husband. Charlie told me to tell you this." They took out a marriage license but never took the final step, perhaps because of whispers that Burton was a gold digger—although it challenges the imagination to find benefits in that relationship.

Manson died unwed on November 19, 2017, one week after his 83rd birthday. He died not on a cross, as his most stubborn followers might have you believe, but in a prison hospital, of the sort of afflictions that we mere terrestrials suffer—colon cancer and a bad heart.

Complete with swastika on forehead, Manson, aged 74, poses for a portrait at the Corcoran State Prison, California, in 2009. The photo was taken to keep his file up to date.

Cocktail of Mental Afflictions

Curious about what the seen-it-all California prison system had concluded about this strange man's delusions and psychopathy, I found a parole report that quoted a 2007 analysis of Manson by Joseph George, a forensic psychologist. The report says: "The inmate indicated that he was not interested in being interviewed for the psychological evaluation." George wrote that "the inmate spoke in a tangential manner" and "attempted to manipulate the process of the interview." He also noted that Manson "has consistently denied any complicity" in the Tate and LaBianca homicides.

Based on Manson's prison medical records, which have been archived over some 60 years, George concluded that Manson showed signs of a list of mental afflictions that could consume three or four chapters of a psychiatry textbook. He began with a "principal diagnosis" of antisocial personality disorder, also known as sociopathy and marked by a lack of regard for right, wrong, and the feelings of others. His second diagnosis was schizotypal personality disorder, which sometimes is found in eccentric oddballs who have no clue about how healthy interpersonal relationships work. George added that Manson exhibited various forms of schizophrenia and paranoia, including the persecution complex about which he never grew tired of preaching.

Paul Watkins, the Jeff Spicoli-style stoner who had the humanity to turn away from Manson when the killings began, died long before the cult leader, in 1990, when he succumbed to leukemia at age 40. In the meantime, he had a family and remade his life as a businessman in Death Valley, where he helped create the local Chamber of Commerce. In his testimony at the murder trials, Watkins made a crucial point that was missed by most of Manson's acolytes, especially those who willingly—gleefully— killed for him. Watkins said, in essence, that Manson was working the Elmer Gantry con straight from the 1927 Sinclair Lewis novel (and 1960 film) that lays out the devious motives of fake evangelists.

"Charlie was always preaching love," Watkins said. "Charlie had no idea what love was. Charlie was so far from love it wasn't even funny. Death is Charlie's trip. It really is."

Resources

Atkins, Susan, *Child of Satan, Child of God: Her Own Story*, Menelorelin Dorenay's Publishing (2011)

Buglioso, Vincent, and Gentry, Curt, *Helter Skelter: The True Story of the Manson Murders*, W.W. Norton (1974)

Cleckley, Hervey, *The Mask of Sanity*, Revised Edition, Mosby Medical Library (1982)

Fromme, Lynette, *Reflexion*, Peasenhall Press (2018)

Guinn, Jeff, *Manson: The Life and Times of Charles Manson*, Simon & Schuster (2013)

Klaw, Spencer, *Without Sin: The Life and Death of the Oneida Community*, Viking Adult (1993)

Lake, Dianne, *Member of the Family: My Story of Charles Manson, Life Inside His Cult, and the Darkness that Ended the Sixties*, William Morrow (2017)

Lofland, John, *Doomsday Cult: A Study of Conversion, Proselytization, and Maintenance of Faith*, Irvington Publishers (1966)

Manson, Charles, and Nuel Emmons, *Manson in His Own Words: The Shocking Confessions of "The Most Dangerous Man Alive,"* Grove Press (1988)

Watkins, Paul, and Guillermo Soledad, *My Life with Charles Manson*, Bantam Books (1979)

Watson, Charles (Tex), and Chaplain Ray, *Will You Die for Me? The Man Who Killed for Charles Manson Tells His Own Story*, Fleming H. Revell (1978)

Index